Move over Mrs Robinson

Move Over, Mrs Robinson

The Vibrant Guide to Dating, Mating and Relating for Women of a Certain Age

Wendy Salisbury & Maggi Russell

ROBSON BOOKS

First published in Great Britain in 2003 by Robson Books,
The Chrysalis Building, Bramley Road, London, W10 6SP

A member of **Chrysalis** Books plc

British Library Cataloguing in Publication Data
A catalogue record for this title is available from the British
Library.

ISBN 1 86105 628 1

Illustrations by Claudia Schenk, © Chrysalis Books plc

Typeset by SX Composing DTP, Rayleigh, Essex
Printed by Creative Print & Design (Ebbw Vale), Wales

For Gabrielle, Lauren and JB, our *raisons d'être*
whether they read it or not . . . best not!

Contents

'I sentence you to 25 years of Gardeners' Question Time, needlepoint and comfy shoes.'

Introduction

Maggi Russell

You will do foolish things, but do them with enthusiasm.
(Colette)

Nowadays, most people die of a sort of creeping common sense, and discover when it is too late that the only things one never regrets are one's mistakes.

(Oscar Wilde)

Life has its difficulties at any age, and as each new staging post in the journey is reached, some things have to be given up so that others can be gained. We reject childish ways in order to be considered adults, we eschew miniskirts in middle-age in order to be taken seriously by garage mechanics. This book is about one thing we single women do not have to relinquish in order to achieve a mature state of grace and wisdom. We're talking about SEX, of course, with all its attendant mysteries.

The passage through middle-age is fraught with tensions, as we traverse a strange terrain of both relief and regret. Relief that we no longer have to go out with so many inappropriate men – regret that fewer of them are actually asking us. We find ourselves entering a paradoxical landscape where there are two forks in the road: the way of the lady of serenity and quiet good taste, or the way of the woman warrior, who must wrestle a new shape out of all that it means to be mature. The trick, of course, is somehow to find a way of combining the two, a Janus-faced persona that is both graceful and feisty at the same time. Janus was the Roman god of gateways and new beginnings. Our modern-day goddess-equivalent, perhaps with a nice practical name like Janet, presides over female journeys, with a face of soulful tranquillity on one side (Estée Lauder discreetly applied), the other with a definite glint of devilry about the eyes.

The main difference between the young and the old is the ability to keep one's options open, and, of course, not getting so damned tired. (Just look how the young find it impossible to commit to *any* event more than a couple of hours in advance, while we like to keep our diaries booked up solid for weeks ahead.) Too many women, on passing forty, also start passing edicts on what is and is not possible any more. While we would agree some things are perhaps no longer tasteful, *possibility* is all a matter of attitude. Perhaps life is not really all that difficult, but nor is it exactly easy. The trickiest bit is handling emotions (all the strife in the world, arguably, comes down to a failing in this department) and it takes courage to do life well.

This book's main aim is to provide some signposts and to dispense some bracing encouragement to all our sisters out there, to fill them up to the brim with crazy bravery. Suffice to say, to do life well from here on we're all going to need plenty of *chutzpah* and downright nerve.

By mid-life, we've all been through some pretty serious stuff. Lady has sung the blues, and boy, were they poignant and bitter-sweet. But now it's time to re-write them to a more up-tempo beat.

Our primary purpose here is to offer an antidote to all the judgemental, societal claptrap out there that says, in a multitude of underhand ways, *that it's unseemly for women over forty to still be sexy.* However, nowhere in this book will you find that awful phrase 'growing old disgracefully'. Grace has everything to do with it, and we would argue that we habitually conduct ourselves with a lot more of it now than we did in our ladette and desperate singleton phases of twenty plus years ago (while we're also having a lot better sex). Therefore, we withhold the right from anyone to judge us until that final day of reckoning when we fully expect the bouncers presiding over Heaven's door policy (the one on the top floor, not the basement gay club) to usher us in on the guest list, with fulsome praise for lives so eventfully and colourfully lived.

Sex still retains pole position on life's list of Greatest Mysteries, right up there with Love, Death, Laughter and why anyone would *choose* a career in colonic irrigation. When young, we are tossed about on the horns of our hormones, mixing up love and lust, confusing commitment needs and insecurity. Now we are older and definitely wiser, we are still mystified by love's wayward ways, but, hopefully, more self-aware, more enquiring and more versatile in our emotional arrangements. And we're all much better at giving and receiving pleasure than before, and definitely don't ever intend to give this up.

Unfortunately, the young would like us to do so. Watching us gaining more and more (love, money, power, shoes) as we go through life we seem to have it all except for snappy skin, shiny hair and supple joints. (These things may seem a hell of a lot to say *Ciao* to, but even if your waistband has become *The Wasteland*, there are many other compensations – trust us on this one.) These infants don't see why we should get to carry on having more sex as well. And they can be extremely judgemental about this.

These Judge Dreads fall into three categories. Younger women (especially daughters) who think we are going to steal their boyfriends and offer them a more fun-filled alternative to marriage; married women our own age who think we are going to steal their husbands; and men our own age who are just downright jealous. The only ones rooting for us (in more than one sense) are younger men, who stand to reap the most benefit from our warm embraces. (Although this book is for single sirens, we do hope marrieds will read it too, so that they can understand what a *jungle* it is out here.)

The Four Rules

There is also this pathetic human need to follow RULES. Ever since the earliest scribes took to memorising clever maxims overheard at dinner parties, and scuttled home to scratch them down on parchment scrolls, a lot of confusing stuff has been handed down about how to understand Love, Sex and Death, mostly in the form of well-meant advice. Humans have been addicted ever since. Most of these rules are about how to get more of the former (Love and Sex) and less of the latter. Some even claim to know how you can avoid dying all together. We have become habituated to relying on pontificating preachers telling us 'How To' do everything properly, rather than trusting what we instinctively know. There's even a book out there called *How To Breathe*.

Well, we promise you this book has no truck with any of that. We all know, you and us and everyone else, as we always have, and always will, what all the answers are to everything. Love, Sex and Death, natch, being absolutely everything. The answers are thus: Love More, Exercise More, Eat Less and Try To Laugh. And THAT'S IT. Absolutely every problem you will ever encounter in your life can be solved by the endless recombining of these four basic rules. Try it for yourself. Workshy? Find some work you Love More. Living beyond your means? Fear Death Less (the number of your possessions being in direct proportion to your fear of death – think about it). Bad thighs? Love them More, Eat Less, Exercise More. Hopeless sex? Find someone you Love More (and probably Eat Less and Exercise More, too, and of course, Try To Laugh.) Fear of Ageing? Love every single thing that moves MORE every minute that you can. Fear of Death? Love More, Exercise More, Eat Less – and LAUGH IN ITS FACE – Ha Ha Ha. Oh yes – and *moisturise*.

So, if we know everything there is to know – what more is there to say? Well, unfortunately, quite a lot. Because we need reminding that all that neurotic babble out there, complicating and confusing everything the way it does, needs hacking down like weeds every now again, just to remind ourselves that absolutely none of it's true.

In its modest little way, this book is dedicated to unmasking just one of the falsehoods among the great salad bar of untruths on offer out there. One that currently concerns the authors greatly and, we suspect, you too – is that older women are no longer sexually attractive, or if they are, they shouldn't be.

A little anecdotal break here to flesh out the point. The other day, a pretty fifty-plus friend of ours was staggering home with six bags of groceries, feeling extremely grumpy and frumpy. She prayed to God for a Good Samaritan. A Hugh Grant look-alike immediately materialised beside her and offered to carry her bags, saying he'd noticed she was struggling. She handed them over gratefully, joking 'Is this part of a twelve-step programme? Like doing a good deed every day, and today's is helping an old lady across the road?' He looked at her quite taken aback. 'No – not at all, you really are extremely attractive.' As they had reached her front door, he offered to carry her bags into the house. She immediately snatched them from his surprised grasp, rushed inside and put the chain on the door, convinced that he must be a pervert. This woman has been seriously brainwashed.

Nothing in life can stay the same for very long. Intrinsic to the fabric of life itself is a propensity for stuff to go out of wack. The very warp and weft of existence is designed to do that. It has to, to keep things fluid, moving, exchanging. You can't capture life, because the nanosecond after a photo of some attractive event has been taken, something starts to disintegrate. Flowers, clouds, moons, pets, people – all wax and wane. The only tragedy is being unhappy about it. We have to face the fact that ultimately we have very little control. At some point in your life a wind will come along, pick you up and dump you down again wherever it chooses. The trick of artful living is to dignify where you land. Likewise, every creature that lives and breathes has its seasons, and every season in nature has its particular beauty – sometimes lush, sometimes austere. Glorify in yours.

Why does our society insist on thinking that our waning years lack glory? That sex is only for the waxing? (Or waxing is only for sex?) That an older woman is not an object of lust? It's too simple to blame the media. They just state as fact, in their moronic way, all the neurotic crap they overhear on buses and in pubs. They turn idle gossip into surveys and reports, then solemnly tell us that five out of ten believe some such bollox. Who are these people? Not any five we know.

Watching jazz *chanteuse* Sarah Vaughan in concert on the Performance Channel recently, we were powerfully struck. She's not exactly easy on the eye. Of indeterminate age (though actually in her seventies, according to an anthology), sweat pouring down over green eyeshadow and heavy jowls, and dressed in a sort of bulky industrial cement sack of black sequins – man – what a woman. No – what a *person*. She doesn't just sing as if powered by atomic fission, she's a veritable big bang. A one-woman weapon of mass destruction. And she's singing about men and heartbreak, and the whole nine yards, and you just know she really understands what she's talking about. Plus you can tell she's still got it all going on. Any teen poppet of today could pose as her chihuahua. This thought gives us pause.

It leads to the realisation that the only other stuff worth watching on TV these days, despite having 98 channels, are re-runs of the *Golden Girls* and *Sex and The City*, which are basically the same show – i.e. paeans to the glory of girlfriends, having sex, and discussing sex with girlfriends. The former twenty-year-old show is more optimistic about life and love for the over fifties woman than anything we see on celluloid today. It sets us wondering why things have gone so seriously awry. A series about four post-menopausal women – none stick thin nor cosmetically enhanced, living together, having lots of laughs, and still dating as many men as possible – would not be made now. The climate has changed radically. Now, the older woman has become even more *déclassée* than ever – ask any Hollywood actress. So what is going on?

True, many of us have lived (just) through some pretty grisly, maniacal, menopausal years. We've all cried a river. But sometime during our fortieth decade, we woke up one morning to find the world that we thought we knew and despised had gone through a subtle shift. Instead of manually peeling our eyelids back, groggy from some hormonally deranged nightmare, we felt a softer wind a' blowing, complete with the answer, my friend. Overnight, with no discernible effort, we've just sort of gracefully *evolved* into older women. *Femmes d'un certain âge.* Yesterday you were tortoise woman, with instep supports. Today Serenity beckons from the foot of your bed, smiling softly in her sky-blue robe. After you've recovered from the shock, the next thing you do is check out what this means. What does this strange, archetypal woman want? To *feng shui* your house? Sell you Avon cosmetics? No, no, no! She is signalling to you that it is time to *move up to the next level . . .* because NOW YOU KNOW WHO YOU ARE. And what you have the right to demand now is higher quality in everything, rather than the old deal with the jumbo economy packs. Along with better bed linen, better cookware and more restrained drinking habits, you also want better Sex and better Love.

Know Your Enemy

HERE is where your dilemma begins. For not only might it be difficult finding anyone out there to have it with, but also there are many out there who actively want to stop you having it. They try to frighten you with bizarre statistics, like there being more chance you'll be blown up by terrorists than find a husband when you're over forty. (OK, don't answer that one.) The sexual older woman can be a terrifying concept, akin to the threat of being harassed by a horny Edwina Currie. (Although there's no doubt that many of Thatcher's cabinet *frissoned* to the sexual charisma of their *lederene*, and spent many a happy hour on the bench fantasising about submitting to a thorough spanking – but then, that's old Etonians for you.)

When the Romans invaded Britain and found all those feisty, busty, metal-brassiered Boedicean matriarchs careering around on the wrong side of the road in their chariots, *sans* MOTs or road tax, they thought, uh oh, we'll soon put a stop to this. Back home they kept wives with complicated hairweaves and designer drapery lolling about on sofas drinking herb tea and bitching, leaving the menfolk free to disappear down to the baths with their rent boys. (Nothing new today in Harvey Nicks, then.) This was the culture they imposed here. No more Celtic battle-axes running amok with broad swords and flaming hair – they'd just breed them out of existence. Refuse to fuck 'em. That would put paid to their wild-eyed ways. Ditto the briefly fashionable medieval witch movement. A bit of enforced retraining through ducking and burning and Wicca soon became *so then*.

It doesn't take a feminist history professor in stilettos to perceive that there's still an up-to-date version of

Witchfinder General going on today. In fact, arguably, today it's all got much worse. Mature, independent women who see themselves as sexy and powerful have a tidal wave of antipathy rushing towards them. But not from the man-in-the-street. Oh no. If you've still got nice hair, a cleavage, or *any* *sort* of bum (thank God there's a man for every conceivable butt geometric), he doesn't care if you're ninety, and probably won't even ask. No – the antagonism is coming from all those with a selfish investment in keeping you a mother figure. Namely women barely out of nappies who now run corporations, ad agencies and the media (of which there are now *millions*), your ex-husband, men your own age, and your own children. And the viciousness of their attacks can be quite alarming.

But the truth is, if we ever liked sex much before the menopause, we may well like it even more now. The pause button is off. *We* want to receive pleasure now, not just give it. If this is a cause for astonishment, it's only because this strange, fucked-up end-of-the-world-as-we-know-it culture would like to dissuade us from such unsuitable ideas, hoping we'll fade quietly away into Creative Writing classes and *Gardeners' Question Time*. The attitude now towards the forty-plus sexually active woman is one of humour or scorn. And words like 'hag' and 'crone', as used by feminist media pundits with misplaced defiance issues, really aren't helping, either. 'Growing old disgracefully' is a ghastly phrase that we repudiate unequivocally, conjuring up as it does a vision of giggling, leopard-skin clad, middle-aged women out on the town, lambada-ing, Mai Tai swilling and toyboy goggling in a horrible Channel 5 type take on the *Antiques Road Show*. Or, before we bury this phrase forever, as seen on *Jerry Springer*, featuring hot-panted grannies, shaking their voluminous booty to the baying crowd, as daughters and grandchildren sink to their knees, keening and rending their clothes with shame.

Never has the need for grace been more apparent than when tiptoeing through the minefield that is mature sex. The sexually active post-menopausal woman is portrayed as either a predatory bitch on permanent heat (Dorien) or a New Age earth mother doing something tantric with a toy boy. Why is the thought of sex and older women so horrible these days – and why has the media now also got it in for older men? Look at the bitchery aimed at Jagger the Shagger. The unpalatable truth is that women of all ages, and nearly all of his exes, are still mad for him at sixty – because he's still sexy, funny, ironic, and up for it with passing models. (Though enough about *him* – he certainly doesn't need our support.) Why does everyone want older people to disappear upstairs on their Stannah stairlifts? Why the horror of wrinkly sex?

We concede that ultimate shriek-fest, *shrivelled genitals*, and that unspeakable horror, *atrophied vaginas*, are not thoughts we dwell on calmly (thank you, HRT). The thinking goes that sex is an animalistic thing, the preserve of all men but only younger women, who are expected to evolve at middle-age into wise bosomy matriarchs. Well, we can do that, and still be sexy, too.

Many men fear the older, controlling woman, the She-Devil herself, quite rightly and sensibly. They want young uber-babes they can dominate in all the nasty demoralising ways they have thought up over the centuries. How can *any* man dominate a sexual, confident, elegant, powerful older woman? It's really not possible (unless he's a cunnilingual genius).

Well, the word is that the Goddess is on her way back into town. Without the breastplate or flaming sword, but bearing the womanly values of grace, compassion, wise judgement and endurance. She is much needed now, in a culture drained and exhausted by the male excesses of corporate greed, exploitation, competition and pornography. It's time to end the collusion, stop trying to compete with men on their own terms. The return of the Lady – not as in ladylike, but as in *Our Lady of Bounty*. The return of the Dame – not as in pantomime but as in *La Belle Dame Sans Merci*. For she can also be strict and forbidding, taking no crap, steely of gaze, withering in retort. The Witch – not of the warty finger, or the New Age clap-trap, but the soulful shakti woman, who may or may not be into herbal healing, but definitely knows how to make a good chicken soup. *Neshama* (a soulful woman), as the rabbis say.

And frankly, they can take back their role models such as certain bewigged and surgically enhanced actresses. These women are becoming indistinguishable from their own male impersonators. And please, please, no more photo-shoots of women we used to love (Julie Christie) or at least admire (Joanna Trollope) sprawled on beds or with legs waving in the air, going on about their new lease of life after surgery/divorce/HRT. We'd much rather think Italian, French – Colette and her boytoy Cheri. We want to think elegant, subtle, understated, mysterious. (Catherine Deneuve, don't you dare do a photoshoot for the *Daily Mail*.) Why do seemingly smart women so often fall into this media trap – that the only way to be deemed attractive is to copy porno poses? Lumley gave us Patsy – but that was satire, for God's sake. Joanna does not really dress like that. Perhaps a few actresses do still amaze us with their youth-fulness – Goldie Hawn, Susan Sarandon – but they were always extraordinarily gorgeous, and God knows how much time and neurosis it takes to keep looking like that. These are not realistic images of the older woman. (Angelica Huston, a tired, soulful, suffering madonna in *The Royal Tenenbaums* – now there's a magnificent, sexy woman, decreed a man we saw it with.)

And we must just say a word about Lulu and Judi Dench. These were women with faces like puddings in their younger days. But it seems under the blancmange lurked wonderful bones. And as the face sunk in, the bones came out, accentuating eyes, nose, chin. Now they are almost beauties.

Looking around at our own forty-plus friends, we find that mostly they look very attractive indeed, and none of them seem to be short of men who think so too. Modern cosmetics, hair products, and diet and exercise know-how have kept us generally fit and well-groomed and, most importantly, we know how to dress. There may still be the odd leather-trouser moment here and there – but we're all entitled to have the occasional ironic lapse. And some women do suit a slightly trashy look. The rule is, pretty women can do tarty – handsome ones will just look like transvestites. (Take all your fashion tips from trannies. Anything you think they might seize from your wardrobe with gleeful cries, cast unto Oxfam forever.) When in doubt just ask yourself, would Charlotte Rampling wear this? The current cultural thinking on what is feminine, as seen in makeover shows (i.e. hooker gear – heavy make-up, hair pieces, push-up bras, short skirts, spike heels) should be left to the babes who can still look both knowing and fresh. Real older beauties go for fine fabrics and maximum coverage – saving revelation for private moments when lovers will be thrilled to discover how unwrinkled and lovely the body remains. (Some true facts here: muscle tone is retrievable at any age, and the skin, if protected from sunbathing, can stay soft and smooth into the seventies and eighties. Generally it's only the neck, hands and upper chest that show ageing, and this is due to weather exposure. Younger sisters – moisturise now!) Those prone to plumpness gain from more youthful skin and voluptuousness. The slender are terminally elegant and sophisticated, and can still wear virtually anything.

But checking again around all these attractive friends of ours, we are also appalled to find how many of them are depressed and on their own. Because the sad fact is that they can't find men of their own age to fall in love with. Where are they all hiding? Surveying the available men we know is not encouraging. Reversing the old status quo, it seems that women really do age better than men. So many (of the latter!) are bald and pot-bellied (not impossibly *outré* per se, but (please!) not coupled with nasal hair or brown teeth). And they can be the bitchiest of all about the ageing woman. These are the people who depress us most.

Before we go any further, we must stress that if this book seems somewhat anti-men in places, we really do still adore, want and need them in our lives. It's just that unless you are tucked up all cosy indoors with your soulmate, it really is a jungle out here, inhabited by snakes who, although they crawl on their bellies, still think that they are kings. There are also ladders everywhere – one minute you are going up, the next you are tumbling down. The dating scene second, third, seventh time around just gets more and more hazardous. By our middle years, we have all been tortured and tormented by the trials of sexual combat in a thousand new-fangled and inventive ways, and are now either battle-scarred and bolshie, or frightened and withdrawn. We all know the old maxim about opposites, like magnets, attracting. Well, they also repel, and many misunder-standings and gross absences of manners go into the battle of the sexes.

In ancient alchemy, a powerful symbol for the force that creates life shows a man and a woman on horseback, locked in eternal combat with dangerous-looking swords. But peer closer, and each bears the likeness of the other on their shields. Modern chemistry tells us that atoms bind with other atoms, which enables them to become compounds. So, at every conceivable level, we are all at it, compounding the night away, from petrie dishes to discos. We don't want to stop binding with men, in or out of the marsh, nor they with us. We have what the other lacks, and yet we are locked in permanent struggle. You don't need the Nobel prize to work out that *this is the way it's meant to be*. Magnetism has an equally powerful negative side. From time to time men are going to seriously get on your tits. Accept it.

This then provides us with an excusable segue into a bit of slagging off. The zeitgeist seems to have created a nasty new vibe to compound our woes. All you lovely women back on the dating scene in middle-age, be warned. Increasingly since the sixties, the excesses of the sexual revolution have caused a kind of ennui in men – a general jadedness about sex altogether. A man will now buy you ONE dinner (and that if you're lucky) and then expect to sleep with you (See Wendy's Bouncing Czech story – pages 54–6). He may assume you are desperate because you are middle-aged and alone. Generally speaking, manners and chivalry have gone out the window. On a second date, a friend (let's call her Molly) went to meet the man at his house (against her better judgement) to find him browsing his favourite (very) hard-core porn sites, expecting her to join in with appreciation. She had never known that women could be so anatomically versatile. She is now quite seriously traumatised. These ex-hippie men are the very worst. Used to chicks who would have sex with them at the drop of a hat, they emerge from long marriages thinking they'll just pick up where they left off.

Unfortunately, the demise of the Lady has done little to stop this impression that all women are, basically, sluts. Older men, now sixty-plus, tend to have better manners generally because they missed out on that flower-power-chick boom, as they were buried in the suburbs. But many men in their forties and fifties now are completely out of touch. Not only do they expect you to sleep with them on a first date, they may also expect you to pay for your own dinner first. We have *things to say* about that. They expect us to drive across town through rush-hour traffic to meet them. They expect us to do kinky things in garish undies. And then they are *still* shy of commitment. They say they've done marriage and kids, and now they just want to have some fun. So go and have it with other men. We women are not *fun*. We are not *sport*. We are about serious, heart-stopping excitement.

Mind you, we do seem to have more fun now than we ever did before, especially when we are with our girlfriends. We have probably never laughed so much, particularly when recounting events that at the time seemed spectacularly painful and bad. The laughter may sometimes have a hollow ring, but it's still a lot better than crying. Mornings after grisly dates, we can become positively hysterical on the telephone, and the worse our experience at the time, the more joy we share in the recounting. A mixture of *schadenfreude* and admiration meets our tales. The Greeks believed that laughter was the sound of the soul expressing its immortal nature, and every human laugh infected the gods above. Humour remains one of life's greatest, and most mysterious, gifts, because although no one can really explain its purpose, when we laugh we do seem connected to a higher realm – time stops and we briefly lose our lonely selves. Reality slips. We can feel quite mad and delirious with joy. Then we are untouchable – and a bad date becomes a source of transcendence.

So this book is for all you vibrant single women out there, who still feel sexy and ready to tango, and who don't conform to the available female stereotypes of matron, earth mother or crone. You know there has to be another option. In fact, we have decided that there are just five basic options, and we have investigated the pros and cons of each one for you, so *you* don't have to (but you can if you like).

1. Toy Boys

Some of us like these, some don't. Some like firm young flesh, being in control and mothering men. If you're still a good-looking woman, it follows that you still want to have sex with good-looking men. You may have to go back anything up to twenty years to find them. (Any longer than this and it starts to look freakish.) And let's face it, no-one should ever have sex with someone they don't fancy, for any reason. (Money, fame, security, pity – unless you're a whore or a saint, there's really no excuse.) Young men are very happy to oblige. The downside is that they rarely stay. Wendy has plenty of enlightening information on this topic. Maggi doesn't like being with men who are prettier than her, and has done enough damage already mothering her own son.

2. Soulmates

Despite all sane evidence to the contrary, Maggi still believes in these. Wendy doesn't (or at least she says she doesn't). Some say waiting for your soulmate guarantees you will stay single forever. Perhaps this is really the whole point. And soulmate seekers never seem happy while they are actually cohabiting with one. Maggi's argument is that it doesn't actually mean not going out with men. It just means surviving hopeless dates by falling back on the theory that one day the self-fulfilling prophecy rule will kick in. People can and do get married again in their sixties, seventies and eighties, much to the chagrin of their offspring. It's worth doing for this result alone. So why not you? Don't go with that crap about it being more likely you'll meet a violent end than get married over forty. These days it's more likely that you'll be caught in crossfire than find a good cup of coffee in the High Street.

3. Sex with friends

Both Maggi and Wendy condone this one. It's what we do
while hunting for toy boys and soulmates. But no-one is
kidding themselves that this is not a cautionary zed-bend
kind of zone. You're hot, romantic and passionate one
minute, the next you're just mates having a ciggie and
discussing David Beckham. It's like the vagaries of the
battery on your mobile phone. One minute you're having a
heated exchange – the next you've gone completely flat.
And only several days incommunicado will charge you up
again. Sex mates are both good and bad. **Good** because you
can have as many of them on the go as you like – and you're
not being a tart 'cause they're not one-night stands (we've
both had ones that lasted a decade). They are by their nature
non-monogamous, and you've always got someone to call
up to take on a date or to respond to a booty call. You
can also fantasise that you *would* be together if only he
wasn't married/Eastern European/a benefit fraudster. **Bad**
because you're going to have to be *very* sophisticated about
this one, and never needy, clingy or possessive, and able to
handle the instability of the whole thing (your booty friend
may absent himself, talk about other women, or fall in love
and leave you at any time, and you're not allowed to make
an ugly scene).

4. Mistresses

This option has rather gone out of fashion these days,
especially since we've become so adept at earning our own
livings in more prosaic ways. It's still a hot ticket in the
higher echelons of society, however, among heirs to the
throne, cabinet ministers, bishops and corporate czars.
Basically, it only works if a married man longs to be
unfaithful, but has a great deal to lose financially and
professionally if discovered, so is willing to pay generously
for your discretion. Flats, furs and extravagant jewellery are

the rewards for your loyalty, handsome payouts by tabloids the rewards for your betrayal. A win/win situation? Materially, maybe, but this is one strictly for the manipulative minxes among us, upon whom, in the spirit of do-as-you-would-be-done-by, we wouldn't dream of passing judgement.

5. All by yourself

This is the state we all return to between bouts of all of the above and – let's face it – where we are all ultimately headed. This has to be coped with, not moped with. In the meantime you have all your other stuff going on – your work, family, friends, hobbies, creative pursuits. Try to see this as some sober practice time. Women generally outlive men whether their husbands were nice or not. Some we manage to kill off – others die in self-defence. We may, perhaps, actually be hoping to drop dead from exhaustion alongside our men folk, like Old Shep. But if you don't, won't you be glad you had all that philosophy in place, fashioned painstakingly out of the lean times, and that you built up that colourful inner life, and a home full of happy memories, and all that sex and love you wrung out of every situation, right down to the last drop.

This, then, is the new 'womanosophy' – the wise way for a woman to live and love. Mature, gracious, generous, loving, but also balancing, limiting, guiding and still a little bit crazy after all these years. *Maktub*, as the Arabs say. It is written. And we hope you will find it makes perfect sense.

'They can't all *be baggage-laden axe murderers with dick problems, can they?'*

1
Dating, Mating and Relating

Wendy Salisbury

Part I

I'm looking for a sensitive, attractive, intelligent man . . . but all those guys have boyfriends.

(Anon)

Those of us in committed relationships, whether they be good, bad or indifferent, spend little or no time obsessing about being single. Those of us who are single spend all of our time obsessing about having a committed relationship. Cohabitees may hanker after their single friends' lifestyles in a grass-is-always-greener sort of way, but they should be aware that grass suffers in extremes of cold and heat. So do humans, and that is the reality of what you have to look forward to when, for whatever reason, you exit a relationship. As an unwilling single, or to put it more bluntly, a dumpee, when you land back on Planet Solo (population 1) you have two options: you can sit at home huddled in a corner hugging a bottle of gin and howling the lyrics to all those love songs, or you can get up, get on with it, and get back Out There. Usually you need to do a bit of both. When I was newly single after a long relationship ended, I could not bear to be home alone. The resounding echo of the silence that surrounded me was just too frightening. Like one of Pavlov's dogs, I'd listen intently for Mr Ex's key in the door at the usual time each evening. My heart would sink to bottomless depths when I realised he wasn't coming back and, to avoid that situation, I'd make sure I was out elsewhere, somewhere, anywhere but sitting solo on the sofa. This escapism was a form of denial: as I soon learned, changing the company you keep or changing your geography does not really change anything. As long as you take the contents of your head around with you, that is all you will focus on, no matter where you are or what you are doing. Women have always had this capacity to do a million things at once under the most tremendous pressure and still be able to think about what ails us (i.e. *him*) 100 per cent of the time. (If *he* is playing pool down the pub, all he is doing is playing pool down the pub.) In the aftermath of a break-up, there will be good days and bad days; accept and embrace them all. The manifestation of grief is a tangible part of the healing process, and if you want to rip his photo to shreds and hurl it in the fire while sobbing your heart out, then go ahead and do it – just don't burn yourself as you scramble to retrieve all the bits. Crying is the most natural form of self-expression. It's our first method of communication as we exit the warmth of the womb. As we grow, it becomes unseemly to emote publicly or privately in such a demonstrative fashion. Sod that. If the brain cannot cope with rationality, a good cry is a cathartic and cleansing alternative. The toxins and poisons released through our tear ducts are nature's way of helping us heal our sorrow. And no one ever died from too much crying, although at the time you may feel that you will. The heart is a mercurial muscle, both delicate and valiant, and able to withstand the gravest trauma or the wildest joy. As long as we take in air and keep on breathing, the heart will do its work and enable us to carry on for one more hour, one more day. Loss is a roller-coaster, complete with its inherent highs and lows, but little by little, day by day, you will feel better. Trust me. I know.

It takes a degree of stoicism and a Degree in Optimism to re-enter the single world with a smile on your face and a spring in your step, but that is the vibe that you must portray. Self-assured self-confidence wins friends and influences people but it's a hard role to play when you just feel like wallowing (poor me, poor me, pour me another drink). The best and quickest way of getting over a broken love affair is to fix yourself up *pretty damn quick* with a new one, even if he comes under the heading of Totally Unsuitable Transition Man. This is a very useful way of boosting your confidence and re-affirming your sexual attractiveness, but should not involve too much emotional investment nor, unless you are very lucky, be thought of as The Next Big Thing. A quick fling with someone you may never see again (Hi M!) can be just what you need to get you through a difficult patch and you'll come out of the tunnel into the daylight, ready to pick up the pieces. A lost love lies like a dead body at a wake dominating the living room of your life, a constant reminder of what was and what might have been. One day you are going to have to bury it. Only then can you begin to start again.

Oh life is a glorious cycle of song
A medley of extemporanea
And love is a thing that can never go wrong
And I am Marie of Roumania

(Dorothy Parker)

Ever since time began, the natural order for anything with a pulse has been to pair off with a member of the opposite sex and form a couple. Despite our modern society of so-called 'self-sufficient singletons' (by 2010, 70 per cent of the population will probably live alone) that status does not fit well into couple culture and is still viewed as a bit of a stigma. The animals went in two by two, and so it seems, must I and you. Without a partner, you are considered to be only half of a potential whole, no matter how high-powered your job, apartment, shoe closet and body maintenance may be. If you are single, you will always be viewed as a bit of a saddo. Self-satisfied marrieds or cosy couples are not quite sure what to do with you. You have lost the acceptance of the tribe by becoming the odd-one-out and the females may start to regard you as a threat. The males will assume that you are permanently gagging for it and will start holding their stomachs in and paying you extra attention whenever you all get together. There still exists the notion that a single woman can be dangerous. (She might be tempted to behave wantonly and steal someone else's mate.) Although friends are happy to sympathise and listen to your tale of woe, they won't necessarily want you hanging around their place being maudlin all the time. Some girlfriends may become over-possessive of their partners, thinking 'there but for the grace of God go I', and this will exacerbate your only-ness and compound your loneliness. Others are only too delighted to act single while still having the security of being in a relationship. They will use your single status as a cover for them to increase their social lives away from their partners and then they'll go and attract all the available men because they're not sending out 'desperate and dateless' vibes like you are. This can be very demoralising. It's bad enough when you are young, but when you have been part of a twosome and are returned to singledom in later life, the problems you thought you would never have to face again return to haunt you, only this time the face has wrinkles.

If they lack optimism and self-confidence, some negative women left alone at a certain age will resign themselves to a solitary and celibate future, believing that the time of romance for them has long since passed, and they'd best begin collecting empty jars lest all that's left for them is to take up jam making. They need to know that *Exposure Equals Opportunity*, so they might want to get out there and expose themselves. When significant relationships end, it is normal to withdraw for a while especially for those who have been tragically bereaved. They wear their sorrow like a shawl and, despite counselling and the healing passage of time, many cannot set aside the grief, guilt and fear of infidelity to their partner's memory that meeting another man would generate. Seeking solace in the bosom of their family is a great comforter and becoming a revered and respected matriarch is a worthy and valuable role, and one that will warm them through the colder days. The nights are another matter, but not everyone wants to replace a late husband, especially if the marriage was a good one. The braver ones move forward and dip a tentative toe into the swirling waters of the social scene – one in which they may not have swum since their teens. Depending on their financial and domestic situation they either need to meet someone else to keep the wolf from the door (providing their settlement or inheritance included a door) or, if they have been left comfortably off, they have to beware of the wolf-like suitors who may come on to them for all the wrong reasons.

Positive women, even those who have been hurt, dumped, lied to or cuckolded, i.e. you, me and everyone else we know, seem to have an amazing capacity for bouncing back. I knew a divorcée with a young son and a day job who was so determined to marry again, she organised dinner parties in other people's houses. She would check out the male guests and swoop like an eagle on any likely lads. Within six months, at age fifty-three, she had met him and married him. Like boxers who have been laid flat in the ring, we scramble on to our hands and knees, struggle up to standing, re-adjust our knickers and go back out there for another ten rounds. We are social goldfish, forgetting past and previous heartaches, as we set off with renewed expectation that the next relationship will be a better one, more enriching, more fulfilling, less of a mind fuck. We keep looking and hoping because to give up is simply not an option.

If having a man around is the missing link between an ordinary life and an extraordinary one, then we must be prepared to work at finding him, and of course, keeping him (assuming we actually want to, once we've got to know him properly). Woman cannot live by bread alone, and sooner or later we get to fancying a nice piece of (beef)cake. If we see him at a bus stop, browsing in the bookshop, queuing at the deli, it is not thought acceptable to make the first move – though several men I have asked say they love being chatted up by vibrant and interesting women. In this sue-ing society where men live in fear of old-fashioned flirting being confused with hard-nosed harassment, they are loath to approach women in the friendly way they once did, but if you register your interest you may well get a positive response. The last thing you want is to have long hairs on your chinny-chin-chin and still be waiting.

There are many more single women out there than men and if he is half-way decent, he can have his pick of the chicks aged from eighteen to eighty. Men know about supply and demand because they get invited to stuff on their own a lot more than we do. No hostess minds having an extra man at her table, no matter that they mostly fall into these categories:

Very nice men who are not handsome.
Handsome men who are not very nice.
Very nice, handsome men who are gay.
Very nice, handsome, straight men who are married.
Ugly, poor men.

Ugly, rich men.
Very nice, handsome, straight, rich men who are called James Bond.

Armed with this information and a Degree in Open-Mindedness from the University of Life, here are some of the ways in which you can meet new men.

. . . education, education, education . . .

(Tony Blair)

Expand your knowledge, broaden your horizons and, *naturellement*, check out the local talent. Reading the prospectus from the local Adult Education Authority can be as entertaining as actually taking the class, a bit like travelling hopefully being better than arriving. Inspiration comes in many forms and below are some of the courses I have attended in the name of research:

Courses
Argentinian Tango: Oh, those haunting rhythms and how hard Juan did hold me. He was the Juan with the black patent hair and white patent shoes whose breath caressed my neck while he pressed his lithe body close to mine. Lost in a passionate embrace, I wanted him to be the only Juan . . . The week before half-term, an over-enthusiastic backbend put paid to all that and I spent the next six weeks sleeping on the floor under the chiropractor.
Flower Arranging: Julian outshone us all with a cheap bunch of freesias and a small twist of chicken-wire. Although this class is not exactly a mate-magnet, I did meet a newly-divorced lady from Basildon who showed me exactly what to do with a sharp pair of secateurs and a fistful of Gucci ties.

Drama and Improvisation: (Normal behaviour – how else do you get through the day?) If you can't act you can produce, direct, prompt or make costumes and scenery. It is also revitalising to become someone else for a while. I slipped effortlessly into a man's tweed suit and a Northern accent, despite the fact that the play was a Sapphic saga set in Sweden. I still like to perform regularly whether required to or not.

Creative Writing: Here you will meet an eclectic mix of aspiring scribes and weirdos you would never normally talk to in real life. One pupil had the hots for the teacher and totally confused 'fuct' with fiction. She catalogued their affair and read the story out in class when he dumped her. Two other students left their respective marriages and ran away together. Who needs make believe? Write on.

Sculpture/Pottery: If you don't mind getting mucky, this is an opportunity to vent your spleen on an indefensible chunk of clay. Inspired by the scene from *Ghost*, I imagined the tutor would stand behind me and skilfully mould my jugs. After 14 weeks, all I'd created was a phallus-shaped lump with a bulbous tip, which I entered in the end of term exhibition under the title: 'Not tonight dear, I've got a headache'.

Keeping in touch with your Inner Child: I was shocked to learn that the balloon I let go of on Brighton Pier in 1952 represented the essence of my lost youth in terms of its spiritual journey into the realms of the universal cosmos, which explains why I cannot read *Noddy at the Seaside* without welling up. Fortunately, both my inner children are now outer children but I do keep in touch regularly by cheque and postal order.

Everyone needs a wife, but I'm not sure anyone needs a husband.

(Germaine Greer)

Dating clubs: Singles rule, OK? No, not really, but there certainly are a lot of us. At the last count, two million Brits were actively looking for relationships through seventy-odd agencies, generating £50m each year. Speed dating is the newest fad, where hard-up hopefuls have up to eight quick-fire dates in one evening before deciding who they fancy the most. You place your tick in the box and e-mail addresses are exchanged. You then have to wait and see whether he fancied you as well. If you multiply 8 × 8, it gives you 64 ways of being rejected, or not, as the case may be. Through necessity, mothering and invention, Introduction Groups, Dining Clubs, Theatre Circles and Friendship Societies have sprung up choc-full of second- and third-time around-ers who have temporarily stepped off the roundabout only to leap back on again with someone else's ex. The women want romance, companion-ship, cruises; the men want sex, home-cooking, listening to. If you are relaxed about it, this form of interactive socialising is an excellent way of increasing your circle of friends while keeping an eye out for a prospective partner. People join all the time, and firm friendships do flourish as everyone is there for a common reason. It is a good idea, however, to remain slightly aloof. Remember that God gave you two eyes, two ears but only one mouth. Look, listen, and observe body language and behaviour. Keep your options open and your legs closed. These places are hunting grounds and meat markets but they do serve a useful purpose, so take what you can from the experience, which may even be a posse of new girlfriends to go around with.

When you meet a new man, never tell him intimate details of your past sex life. He will judge you by them and assume that because you've done 'all that' you're definitely up for doing it all again NOW. With him. No man loves you for yourself. He loves you for himself.

Anything else he says is a phallus-y. Here are some tips if you are a first-timer at a Singles Social:

- Observe the male – if he flits from woman to woman like a bee at a flower show, he is probably only looking to make honey.
- Never go in wearing your 'I am The Huntress' T-shirt as this will alienate the other ladies, plus, although you may get loads of sex, you are unlikely to find true love and respect once you have been passed around the group like an old bicycle.
- If a man asks for your phone number, ask for his instead. If he only gives a mobile or a work number, he may be married. I knew a married guy who trawled the singles scene picking up women, in that arrogant way they have of assuming that if you are not actually married, you are desperate for a shag. In my experience, it's the married women who get less sex than us singles do.

Use these events as stepping stones to new adventures, because even if you don't meet Mr Right, his nemeses Mr Cheap, Mr Boring and Mr Fat Bastard may have other friends to whom you could be introduced.

The Book Group: This is a dating agency for the erudite. Hardly anyone actually ever reads the book, but you get to see the inside of other people's homes with free tea and biscuits thrown in. The literati who take it seriously are intensely crusty with overgrown toenails and grey pubes, though I state this from imagination rather than experience.

Personal aQs: *'Horny hunk hung like hippo wanted now'.* You want to buy or sell something, what do you do? You advertise it. Your house, your car, your products, your services, so why not yourself? This written form of mate-meeting is now available in every publication from *Halibut Fryer's Monthly* to *The Abseiler's Gazette*. Called Affairs of the Heart, Encounters, Personal Touch, Tryst, Meeting Point or Duet, no matter what the wording says, what it really means is: I need a cuddle. And it has a long history, Adam being the very first lonely heart. I think his personal ad (in *Spare Rib*) must have gone something like this:

> *Solitary bachelor, no baggage, likes naturism and gardening, WLTM soulmate for snake-charming, apple-picking and maybe more.*

My cynical side believes that there ought to be one big magazine simply called *Pigs 'r' Us*, because no matter how carefully chosen the words are, this is one area in which honesty is the worst policy, although here are some (supposedly) genuine adverts from a magazine in Ireland:

- *Bitter disillusioned loser lately rejected by long-term fiancée seeks decent, honest, reliable woman if such a thing still exists in this cruel world of hatchet-faced bitches.*
- *Ginger-haired trouble-maker, gets slit-eyed and shirty after a few jars, seeks wealthy lady for bail purposes, maybe more.*
- *Bad-tempered foul-mouthed old bastard living in a damp cottage in the arse end of Roscommon seeks attractive 21-year-old blonde with big tits.*

Selling yourself is the hardest pitch of all – try writing your own advert and you'll see. And who can help but bend the truth? The follically challenged, overweight pisshead who laughs at his own jokes becomes *'Well-built Bruce Willis-type with GSOH and degree in viniculture'*. The dumpy, peroxided short-arse with rotten teeth sells herself as a *'Petite*

Rubenesque blonde with shy smile'. If all the males who
advertise are really tall, dark, handsome, fit, sensitive, solvent, professional, loving and cultured, and all the women
are beautiful, slim, erudite, curvaceous, tactile, sensual and
passionate, why the fuck haven't they got someone? Some
lucky advertisers do find each other and this is a rare and
wonderful thing. Like old-time pen pals, geographically
unsuited hopefuls can build up secure and trusting
attachments learning everything about each other long
before they meet. Then, if the chemistry is right, they've
done the hard bit, formed a mental liaison and can get on
with the pleasure of the physical one. Of course, their
grown-up children will heartily disapprove (what goes
around comes around) because they believe that their
parents should be with each other and no-one else. They are
also disgusted by the idea of 'crinkly' sex and are much
agitated by the matter of the inheritance falling into the
wrong hands. Never mind them, they've got their whole
lives ahead of them to make their mistakes, we're running
short of time to carry on with ours.

Personal Introduction Consultants (*what used to be called Marriage Bureaux*)

These have a very valid social role in today's society. As we
all lead such busy lives and many of us live in isolation in
inner cities, unless we meet someone in the workplace or are
introduced by friends, we do not always have the time to
network the scene looking for love. In the same way that an
estate agent finds you a house, an accountant handles your
finances, a solicitor advises on law, for a fee, a dating agent
finds you a partner. Or that's the idea. Once you have
registered and told them your inside-leg measurement,
wheat and dairy intolerances and how many hours a week
you don't spend at the gym, their database will go into
matchmaking overdrive trying to find your perfect mate.

They also sort through the dross for you, which saves time but denies you the dubious pleasure of The Disastrous Date (see Part II). You can go back as many times as you like to trawl through pages of photographs, videos and profiles, and once you have made your selection you can fix up that all important Date. When you arrange to meet for the first time, keep it casual, just go for a drink or even a walk. You may have clicked over the phone, but if there's no vibe when you are face to face, you don't want to waste a whole evening wondering why he grew his nose hair so long or listening to him droning on about what a bitch his ex-wife was but how he got custody of the cat. (If you don't know the man, play it safe. Tell someone where you are going and have them call you 30 minutes into the date to check you're OK.)

Online Love: . . . *you'll never know my bad hair days, nor I your irritating ways* . . . (WS)
I bet Bill Gates never had himself pegged as Cupid, but the World Wide Web is no longer an uncommon place in which to meet someone. It is the fastest-growing romance, match-making and dating service in existence, offering to bring millions of virtual people into your home at the push of a button. Which means you don't have to shave your armpits or tidy up. It is easy, anonymous and free and there is an ever-increasing choice of new recruits every minute of every day. There are chat rooms set up for all ages and sexes, and if you have a special hobby or fetish you can set up your own. If you find you have a particular connection with someone, you can go one-to-one for a more intimate talk. If you fancy, you can have a one-night stand with a total stranger (just like in the old days) or progress to a meaningful relationship and even marriage. Some sites are split into categories: Casual Dating (for those seeking companionship), Romance or Long-term (if you're looking to settle down) and Intimate Encounters (if straight or deviant sex is what you're after).

The e-nonymity of an online affair provides the lovers with the same flirtatious *frissons* as any other romantic involvement. With blushes spared by the absence of eye contact, the most timid of typists can reveal themselves in a much less restricted way. We have all experienced higher confidence levels on the telephone where we don't have to expose our visible vulnerabilities. And cybersex is safe sex. No bodily fluids are exchanged. Enter and Send have taken on new meaning, as he no longer needs to enter your bed chamber to send you into raptures of delight. You can sit there in your thousand-times washed grey bathrobe with something wildly organic going on below the waist and if you don't tell him, he ain't never gonna know. For these infatuations are fuelled by the power of imagination.

For some, chat rooms have become the new discos, wine bars and pubs, and you wouldn't think twice about giving your phone number to someone you'd only just met in those alcohol-fuelled environs. Online, you need never leave the comfort of your own keyboard, and there are an increasing number of success stories. Marriages are made in cyberheaven. My own surrogate daughter, a beautiful, intelligent, sexy thirty-two-year-old, who has been let down more times than a whore's drawers, joined an online dating service and just got married to an eligible, gorgeous, and very, very normal man. Respect K. & D.!

Michael, a retired widower, with much life and love left to give but far too timid and out of practice to go out looking, met Christine, a divorced head teacher, on a Friendship Site and they are now engaged.

Bob, a police inspector, whose working hours were too erratic to socialise, met Irene, a nurse, with a similar schedule and they are planning their wedding to the delight of all their friends and family.

These real-life romances are not to be scoffed at. If they can do it, so can you.

Imagination is the highest kite one can fly.

(Lauren Bacall)

One of the problems with internet romance is that you are surrounded by the illusion of honesty and openness. *Roget's Thesaurus* describes cyber as 'fake, virtual, replicated, pretend'. Bear this in mind if you are e-mailing, and don't assume that what you are getting is a true view of someone else's life. Are you telling him the truth, the whole truth and nothing but . . .? There is a lot of role play going on and you may fall in love with an image rather than a real person. As Stendhal said:

> *'Love has very little to do with the beloved person and everything to do with the lover's imagination. Nothing is so seductive as our own thoughts; the passion that sweeps us off our feet is our own.'*

As in real life, it is better not to rush into anything. Internet romances should lead to real relationships, which last long enough for the people involved to really get to know each other and allow time to strip the façade that may have been created. You may have fallen in love with his words (think Cyrano de Bergerac) and created a brilliant picture of him full of hope and expectation, but try to temper that positivity for fear of disappointment.

Like any potentially intimate activity, chat rooms and online dating services come with a Government Health Warning. To sign up you have to choose a fictitious name and secret password. You are warned never to reveal your true identity, nor to give out any personal data. Never arrange to meet anyone unaccompanied, or without letting someone know where you are going. Abuse, harassment and threats exist online as well as off. Although he said he was a thirty-eight-year-old investment banker he may in fact be a sixty-eight-year-old incestuous wanker. Opportunists and creeps stalk the cyberstreets looking for needy, vulnerable victims so beware and be aware. Hearts have been broken when 'friends' have disappeared from your screen, usually when their partners discover that they are not investing in the Hong Kong Stock Market at 3a.m. but playing plastic fantastic with big-breasted Brenda from Brisbane. Gender re-arrangement is another hazard. A slim eighteen-year-old brunette from West London called Mandi turned out to be a 20-stone, fifty-year-old long-distance lorry driver from Wigan called Maurice.

If you do progress to a relationship, waiting for an e-mail provides exactly the same anticipatory thrill or hand-wringing wretchedness as waiting for the phone to ring. You check your messages constantly and the temptation to contact him the e-way is as strong as any other way. But once you've pressed that Send button, there's no turning back. You send it, he gets it and it can only be from you. No withheld number, no hanging up. And don't think for one moment that your private e-ntimacies are your own affair. There's no little key with this diary. He may be copying your relationship to any number of contacts. A recent saucy summary of a long, lascivious lunch was (h)e-mailed round the office. By the time everyone had forwarded it to their friends, 20,000 people around the globe knew exactly why Louise got back late with her knickers in her handbag and spent the afternoon squirming in her chair while perched gingerly on one buttock.

It is very easy to get carried away with a super-sounding e-mate and for those of you who want a man in your life but not in your home, online love may be the ideal solution. You can drag it out for as long as you like, keeping his interest aroused with a catalogue of true (or false) fascinating facts about yourself. You can play hard-to-get and wind each other up, just like in a real relationship. You can remain anonymous and in control. The sex can be fabulous, inventive, abandoned, for your most powerful erogenous zone, your mind, will play a crucial part in your love-making, while all you have to do is learn to type with one hand and let your fingers do the walking. When you've finished, you get the whole bed to yourself and no snoring. Sounds perfect to me.

Have I Got a Man for You!

The safest way to meet someone new is through a personal recommendation. When you first return to the social scene as a second-hand single, well-meaning friends and relations rally round and mastermind introductions to other shelf-dwellers of their acquaintance like 'that very nice chap, Norman, from Accounts', who, like you, happens to be free to attend their dinner party on Saturday night. Partly because 'you never know' and partly to please them, you arrive on time all done up like the 4th of July and your heart skips a beat as your eyes light on Gorgeous Gary who just happens to be . . . with someone else. Norman is usually the sad dork in the corduroy jacket who may be a very nice man, but still looks like Mr Bean, even after three vodka tonics and half a bottle of Beaujolais. You will probably accept a date with him to please your friends and he may be a charming companion for a movie, dinner or museum outing. Alternatively, you could end up playing hide the salami in the cupboard under the stairs with Gary while his wife spends the evening banging on about the complexities of completing Luke's UCCA form and how she and Gary never seem to have sex any more.

Sweet Solitude

If you have a hobby or a subject that has always fascinated you, use your newly-reclaimed evenings and weekends to learn more about it. This may mean going to lectures on

Early Gothic Architecture or joining a walking group on a Historical Tour of Little Venice. Either way, you will meet other people with a similar interest and get some brain food and exercise at the same time. Museums and art galleries are culturally stimulating and perfectly acceptable places to visit on your own. Keep your eyes open for esoteric intellectuals staring pensively into the middle distance. Find one you like the look of, sidle up beside him and emit a deep sigh or a sensual moan in front of the oeuvre he is studying. This could well provoke a response, which might lead to a conversation, a cup of tea and a buttered scone in the Museum Café, followed by the possibility of deconstructing Degas in his hotel room or house in Hampstead later that same afternoon.

When there are no men around, live like one.

(Anon)

If you've tried every angle and love has still not come your way, think about the up side of being on your own. You can slob around all weekend in mismatched undies and your favourite fat clothes. You can eat peanut butter straight from the jar with your finger like you used to when you were twelve. You can play your music, do your crossword and talk to your friends without fear of attention-seeking or interruption. You can spread henna on your hair and mashed avocado on your face and lie in bed flipping channels to your heart's content. That's usually when that horny new neighbour from across the hall comes round to borrow a cup of money. Try to look cute or cock a deaf 'un. Either way, he'll only be aggravation and you've had your share of that.

'You could toss your own in for good measure, Malcolm, but I'm never going to fancy you . . .'

Part II

Send in the Clowns

Men are like fine wine. They start out like grapes and it's a woman's job to stamp on them and keep them in the dark until they mature into something you'd like to have dinner with.

(Anon)

This book would not be complete without a bit of a rant, and this is it. When Maggi and I first started our never-ending discussions about the opposite sex and why they behave the way they do, she was more generous towards them than I was, and criticised me for being 'too down on men'. Sadly, after a few more disastrous dates with crappy cowards, she has rapidly sunk to my level and has, in fact, overtaken me in the 'why do men have to be such a brain fuck?' debate. Why do they bother to say they will call, when they have no intention of doing so? Why bother to make a date and then cancel at the last minute, or (you know who you are . . .) just not turn up? Why bother to carry on breathing when you're just taking up space on the planet that could be more productively allocated to a Rwandan gorilla? We know that the genders do not share the same agenda. We know that although we are all looking for the same thing, i.e. love and happiness ever after, there are those who have a pretty shitty way of going about it. No matter how we long to live in harmony, keep our cool, our serenity, accommodate and commiserate, some men just don't get it. Maybe they are punishing their mothers for closing the bedroom door and leaving them in the dark, their ex-wives for withdrawing conjugal rights and all the money from their joint bank accounts, and every woman who ever rejected them without giving a valid reason (like we need to!). Maybe it's simply the fact that their penises don't come up to scratch, or don't come up at all . . . go figure. We try to cherish and understand them, make allowances for their failings and foibles, cajole instead of criticise, boost their confidence whenever possible, but some self-styled 'dishes' seem to contain MSG or e-additives that initially enhance their basic make-up but later leave you feeling twitchy, irritable and sick to the pit of your stomach. From someone who has suffered at the hands, in the cars, on the couches and in the homes of more bastards than unmarried parents ever gave birth to, my advice is this: do not pour good love after bad. If it isn't working after a decent crack at it, it probably never will. Take a deep breath and MOVE ON. Do not let them live rent-free in your head. Do not let them diminish you nor steal your peace of mind. It is their insecurities and inadequacies that make them try to reduce you in order to augment themselves. Do not dwell, agonise or obsess. Stay focused on the future and concentrate on remaining whole. And keeping busy. Easy? No, it isn't. But there comes a time when enough is enough. Phew . . . I feel better now.

The secret of a successful single social life is to collect as many people around you as possible, both male and female, animal and vegetable, in order to fill your days and nights with infinite variety. This will involve getting your potato off the couch and making the effort to seek out old friends and cultivate new ones. Your hunter-gatherer should have been amassing admirers since you first became aware of *la différence* at around age three, when your *femme fatale* gene kicked in and taught you that eyelash-fluttering and a coy smile go a lot further than tears and tantrums in endearing yourself to the opposite sex. Four or five decades later, the same principles apply, so with time and dedication, searches and sorties to the variety of venues suggested in Part I of this chapter, you should by now have a selection of suitors to install in your stable. Being socially lazy and not generally a'brim with original ideas, most men rather welcome being led in a 'I hear there's a marvellous new play at The National' kind of way. Like a horse whisperer, you can insinuate suggestions into their shell-likes then act surprised and delighted when they produce the tickets, making them believe it was all their idea. If you do not keep them moving around the public parade ground, they will remain in their stable watching TV and eating hay until the next suggestive mare comes along. There *will* be the odd stallion who must be ridden at least twice a week lest he become twitchy and liable to bolt. Of course he will bolt occasionally, usually into the arms/beds/kitchens of other women from his past, present or future, but having served the marriage sentence and finally got your parole, you may not actually want anyone around full-time.

Part-time temping in a dating context, as any good secretary will tell you, gives you the opportunity to survey the scenery without committing yourself full-time to any of it. You may meet a chap who likes jazz, another who goes to Salsa, a third who's a vintage film buff and a fourth who cooks couscous every other Thursday. These are the men with whom you can have a varied and active social life without them having their fingers in your pie and their laundry in your basket. The sex issue will have to be addressed individually according to merit – only you can be the judge of that. In any new relationship it will become an issue sooner rather than later, and it will certainly have been on their minds within seconds of meeting you. When to go to bed with someone is probably one of life's most F.A.Qs, so obsessed are we with The Rules of sexual tactics and getting the timing right. Too soon and you're branded easy, too late and they'll think you're frigid. Eve probably deliberated the matter even as she was offering Adam the apple, but she wasn't exactly spoilt for choice. There are some men with whom the chemistry is so hot that you jump each other's bones first and introduce yourselves later (rarer than a cuddly porcupine). With others you need to build it up like an orchestral symphony, one note at a time, leading to the big crescendo. There is a third group of perfectly nice blokes who simply will never ring your bells, even if they turn up covered in chocolate with an Amex Centurion card in one hand and a Harry Winston package in the other (although on that basis, I could be swayed). I had a date with a man who turned up wearing a Freddie Krueger mask. The awful thing was that when he took it off he didn't look that different – in fact, the mask gave him a certain sinister, sexual *quelque chose* that the real face didn't. Unfortunately, men do not want to be 'just good friends'. After a few dates with no more than a goodnight peck, their patience runs out and you either have to deliver the goods or wave goodbye. They have a problem understanding the word 'platonic' – it does not feature in their dick-tionary. By declining their advances, you are in danger of losing them altogether. But to submit against your body's will and judgement, just because he's bought you a few dinners, is an unappetising way to end an evening. If you really enjoy a man's company but simply cannot bring yourself to sleep with him, try politely suggesting (sincere eye contact and comforting hand on arm here) that what you two have is far more valuable and enduring, and you wouldn't want to jeopardise a wonderful friendship just for the sake of sex. Admit that you find him terribly attractive but you are:

(a) trying celibacy to purge yourself of the damage done by a previous boyfriend,
(b) afraid your pelvis has a habit of locking at inopportune moments or

(c) have just had a small op 'down there' which means you are out of action for the moment.

Suggest you continue as friends and that he take up one of the hundreds of other offers he undoubtedly gets elsewhere. He will be in turn flattered and clueless as to what you're talking about. It's worked for me on several occasions and I have some excellent male-mates in my stable, but I lost a friend of 25 years' standing by reluctantly succumbing to his drunken advances one fateful night thus ending our long and treasured relationship in an awkward fumble of mutual embarrassment and regret. (Hi, O.)

Men who have been single for a number of years, be they bachelors, divorcés or widowers, will have become set in their own particular ways. Some will be so jaded by the dating game that they retreat into a world of familiarity and comfort, in which there are no mysteries, miseries, nor mammaries: poker, football, dog-walking, male voice choirs. Others, the socially-successful ones, are harder nuts to crack as they will always fancy themselves more than they fancy you. You will probably come across both genres in your travels, and if a prospective partner who knows he's eligible is presented to you, you may need to grab him before someone else does. This is a bitch-eat-bitch world, so take a lesson from our proactive younger sisters and if he doesn't call you, call, text or e-mail him. I know it goes against the grain of us twenty-first-century women with our twentieth-century ways, but sometimes you have to chase a man until he catches you. If you don't do it, someone else will, or he might, as I recently heard, bump into his childhood sweetheart and marry her because it's less hassle than having to start from scratch with you.

Move Over, Mrs Robinson

The best love affairs are those we never had.

(Norman Lindsay)

The best bit about a date with a new man is the build-up, the anticipation, the flirtation in your imagination. The event itself rarely lives up to the flights of fancy we embark on in our airy-fairy heads pre the actual moment of impact. Lying in a scented bubble bath pampering our bodies with all the dedication of a Home Farm organic poulterer, we mentally transmute ourselves into a sex goddess with perfect skin, hair, teeth and nails beckoning from the portal of our gracious abode in a wafting silk gown with matching Manolos. He arrives on a white steed (or, please God, a navy Bentley Turbo with cream leather interior) clutching a bouquet of hand-dyed cala lilies in one hand and a bottle of Dom Perignon rosé in the other. He whisks you off to a moonlit rooftop overlooking a starlit city where a candlelit table is laid for two. An orchestra plays your favourite love songs and he proposes over a dessert of non-fattening cream-filled strawberry meringues . . . Reality check! The doorbell rings and you are still in the throws (sic) of tipping your entire wardrobe on to the bedroom floor in a futile attempt to find something to wear that does not accentuate your expanding *tuchas*, thickening ankles, drooping boobs, double chin. You still have one large roller in your fringe and a glob of mascara just south of your left eye. You haven't had time to do your nails, and the scented candle you bought in the market smells like leg wax and hasn't got a wick. He's stood there in his trying-to-look-ten-years-younger jeans, which fail to conceal a lifetime's dedication to fermented hops, and an aroma which he thinks says 'testosterone' but you interpret as 'nosoapathome'. Of course all men, whether young, old or indifferent get confused as to what is expected of them. They seem to think that a fascinating first date involves them telling you the unexpurgated version of their life story. Fascinating for them, maybe. You'll be sitting there smiling and nodding, while thinking up ways to fake your own death. The insipid ones can be bum-numbingly boring, the cocky ones too full of bravado, bravura and braggadocio. Some are so busy boasting bollox that finding areas of compatibility is like searching for Pavarotti's *pipik* – you know it's there some-where but is it actually worth the look? I once exited a restaurant after dinner with a very handsome TV Producer who had monopolised the entire evening with tales of his own success. Once on the pavement, I stared him straight in the eye and said: 'So, Mark, I know everything about you, what do *you* know about me?' His tortured expression was the only laugh I had all evening.

At some point, once we have been round the block a few times, we may decide it's time to settle, and if so, for what? Are we ready to accept that at our age and at this stage, Mr Mediocre-Who-Will-Pay-For-Hip-Replacement-Later-On is the best we're going to get? Or is it worth waiting and hoping just in case Mr Where-Have-You-Been-All-My-Life comes along? Despite a lifetime of dodgy dates and excruciating experiences, I have to believe the latter.

God gave men a brain and a penis but only enough blood to run one at a time.

(Robin Williams)

As more and more marriages fall apart and September singles spill back out on to the social scene, dating in later life becomes more complicated than at any other time. In the male later-dater, age and experience are not an endorse-ment for mature behaviour. Their sexual evolution and cerebral development remain arrested somewhere between the nursery (nipples and nappies) and the top shelf of the newsagents (nipples and *noonis*). They may look all grown-up with their long trousers and hairy ears but they are really just little-boys-lost in a world of commerce and commitment. These ageing adolescents also have very strong views as to how an evening out should end, i.e. 'the trade-off'. Many presume it is their right, having stumped up for dinner once or twice, to count on their date as being dessert, reasoning thus: two meals, say £100, pretty much what you would expect to pay an average hooker. As far as women are concerned, there is no trade-off. We offer the pleasure of our company and nothing more, unless we choose to. But for he who pays the bill there is an assumption, an expectation, a demand even for sexual favours in exchange for food. This probably goes back to some primeval prehistoric pact that took place in a cave One Million Years BC. It equates to gorillas bringing bananas to the female camp. By way of a thank you, they got to pick nits out of their girlfriends' groins on day one and this information has filtered down through the male's I.T. system and left an indelible imprint. Well, sorry, mateys, but we don't actually have to forage for food any longer – all the big supermarkets have online ordering and delivery services, so there. I have been in this situation many times, even to the point of smacking one predator's gob with the riposte: 'What makes you think that buying me dinner gives you the right to stick your tongue down my throat? If you want your dinner back, I'll gladly oblige!' (fingers via tonsils). He was so taken aback that he conceded defeat and, once I'd explained that I liked him very much – though not in a physical way – and that lovers come and lovers go but good friends last forever, he agreed to be friends and so we have been these past fifteen years. On his fiftieth birthday, he consulted me about dropping his juvenile nickname of Bobby, thereafter to be addressed by his given name of Robert. 'Oh,' I laughed, 'and I suppose you'll want your dick to be referred to as Richard?' Bobby he was and Bobby he stayed.

Ask any older single woman about her dating history and you'll hear some horror stories that Hammer would have been 'Proud to Present'. In fact, you'll wonder if it isn't smarter to carry a hammer instead of a handbag. When you meet someone in your teens/twenties, your overall require-ments are simple and undemanding. He's got to be fanciable, wear the right kit and not skin up in front of your parents. As you grow older and more worldly-wise, the criteria upgrade to: own business, own teeth, retention of marbles and enough in his pocket to buy theatre tickets and the odd dinner (more about odd dinners later). Impeccable personal hygiene, a GSOH, a generous nature, a dashing dark side, an entertaining raconteur and an attentive listener are also high on the list of priorities. We offer all these attributes along with wit, wisdom, beauty, grace, insight, compassion, charm and prettily painted toenails, so why on earth shouldn't they?

I've had a wonderful evening but this wasn't it.

(Groucho Marx)

We have to face the fact that the male of the species generally does not age very well. Despite the availability of the gym, the diet sheet, the electric nose-hair trimmer, they tend to slouch, slurp, develop paunches and become hirsute in uncalled for places. In general, it would be infinitely better if they kept their clothes on for, beneath the cloth, be it cotton or cashmere, Adonis has become Adonisn't, omnipotent is now homme impotent, and where once you lay prostrate, now it's his prostate. A trophy is facing atrophy. In my colourful career as a non-selective single lady since 1986, I (WS) have had more dates than an Arabian palm tree. To amaze, amuse and to serve as a warning to you all, I highlight below a selection of the species:

Homo Antiquus Depressus: This poor old geezer wears a

cardigan with elbow patches and grey synthetic shoes. He's signed the big house over to her (things were never the same since she came back from that Cookery Course in Tuscany crowing about how Luigi tossed his mussels) and he now lives in a rented hovel with someone else's furniture and an inherited smell of must. He did, however, retain custody of his collection of china clowns, so all is not lost. His idea of foreplay is not double-knotting the tie cord on his pyjama bottoms. His specialist subject is hypochondria, and his afflictions outnumber the ten plagues of Egypt. If you fancy a future filled with hospital visits and detailed dialogues over dinner about the merits of haemorrhoid cream and ear wax dissolver, this is the man for you.

Homo Juventus Ridiculus: This one thinks that 'newly single' means 'cool dude'. Like that expression, he went out of fashion in the seventies. His wife kicked him out for shagging the switchboard operator (don't they ever have one original thought?) and now he's reverted to behaving like Jack the Lad. In truth, he's Jack the Sad, but when he looks in the mirror, the passage of years melt away and he still sees himself in the seventies. So he squeezes his expanding arse into a new pair of Levis and, because he's an accountant, he buys himself a Harley Davidson, which any street-wise female knows affirms his ever-decreasing ability to achieve and maintain a full erection. Then there's the barnet question: does he honestly believe that if he combs it all over to one side, you'll actually think he's still got some? And what does the baseball cap say? Complete Tosser? The ensemble is topped off with a leather bomber jacket intended to establish him as a 'total babe magnet'. Not! He dates a succession of twenty-five-year-old shop assistants that he hits on in the bar at The Sanderson, but one fateful night while performing his usual routine, he fails to get it up. He buys himself a state-of-the-art laptop so he can order Viagra online and was last seen circling the marital home like a hungry vulture watching his ex-wife coming and going with her new younger boyfriend.

Homo Suavus Monte-Carlos: What marks this one out from the rest is that his attractiveness is in direct proportion to his bank balance. He is impeccably turned out from the top of his silver-rinsed head to the tips of his Berluti-clad toes. He can get a table at Le Caprice for tonight where he regales you with tales of the length of his yacht, the names of his polo ponies and his penchant for hostile takeovers. After a few drinks, you manage to convince yourself that you really could fancy him – until that fatal moment when he slides out from between the sheets to visit the loo (didn't he just go?) and you catch sight of his baggy old bum disappearing into the distance . . .

Despite this slightly twisted view of mine, I feel it only fair to say that I know there are some flawed but lovely men out there, and I am fortunate enough to be friends with a few of them. No matter how fulfilled we are in every other aspect of our lives, they still have the edge as some primitive inbred message informs us that we can never be completely whole unless we have that other half, that missing link, that absent piece, that mate, that partner, that much-maligned but much-loved extension to our single selves: a man – the Adam to our Eve, the Romeo to our Juliet, the Napoleon to our Josephine, the Prince Charming to our Cinderella. So, in true princess-style, we know we have to kiss a lot of frogs. And assholes.

Here are some of them – only the names have been changed to protect the guilty:

Richard the Turd

Daisy met this Dick on the Internet. They got on swimmingly, exchanging life stories, love stories and intimate personal anecdotes. She felt she knew him well

enough on every level and so a *diner à deux* was arranged.
He arrived late at the pre-arranged venue having had to
'wait for a bus' (minus ten points). A drink-driving ban was
later admitted (minus fifty points). The evening was going
quite well until he went into one of those pocket-punching
moments when the bill arrived. Daisy had no alternative but
to produce her credit card and pay for the lot. He suggested
they stop off at his office on the way home so he could pick
up some cash to reimburse her. He hailed a taxi, mumbled a
destination and leapt out on arrival telling her he would be
'back in a minute'. After 20 minutes with the clock ticking,
Daisy realised she would never see him again . . .

The Creep from Colindale

Lisa should have known when he told her his address that
this character spelled trouble. He lived in an area famed
for its one-parent families where the *pater* is *in absentia*
usually resting At Her Majesty's Pleasure. But he had an
engaging smile, an upbeat manner, and more front than
Woolworth's. Just what she needed after her rough
divorce. He also had a dark side, but just how dark Lisa
was yet to find out. She was renting a flat before finding
somewhere permanent to buy with her settlement monies.
He registered the lump sum earning interest like a fox
registers the whereabouts of a rabbit. He too was 'renting',
or perpetrating a mortgage fraud, or something. He didn't
appear to have a job as such, but boasted of import and
export – designer watches, ethnic comestibles, cartons of
tobacco. It stank, but Lisa couldn't smell it. Not yet. Within
weeks, he came up with a property deal: go halves on a
cheap flat, do it up, share the profit. She agreed, but at the
eleventh hour he failed to produce his half. He chipped in
a small borrowed amount and they completed the purchase
in her name. He then proceeded to rip the place apart,
appropriating the roof space to create another floor without

landlord's consent, planning permission nor building regulations from the council. She kept asking if he knew what he was doing but he assured her he'd done this many times before. (Funny he wasn't in jail . . .) Lisa was funding all the works. He occasionally turned up with a black eye or a grazed fist saying he'd hurt himself on site. It later emerged that he was being chased and beaten up fairly regularly by creditors. On the completion of the refurbishment, the flat was marketed and a profitable sale agreed. The champagne flowed, but Lisa felt uneasy, and rightly so, because when the original lease plan reached the solicitor, in no way did it match the new extended layout. There then ensued two years of sleepless nights, monstrous expense and hand-wringing anguish, from which Lisa thought she would never recover. She had to pay £10,000 for the roof space. She had to pay £29,000 for remedial works. She had to negotiate with district surveyors, architects, planners, freeholders, managing agents and lawyers to save her dwindling savings and her skin. They threatened to sue for appropriation. They requested she reinstate the flat to its original condition. They demanded she install an alternative means of escape in case of fire – in the form of another staircase enclosed inside fireproof walls. She had to move in to the property she had grown to detest because her rental was up and she had nowhere else to live. The culprit kept a low profile, since they were no longer on speaking terms. Then Lisa began to get threatening letters from him. He wanted to sue her for the return of his contribution plus a profit share and payment for works undertaken. *HALLO?* Lisa became afraid to open her mail since it invariably contained a bill, a threat, a demand or a legal document. Through a concerned friend, she found out that he had recently been declared bankrupt and was not entitled to the legal aid he had falsely obtained to take her to Court. She stood her ground and eventually he gave up. She stayed in the flat for five years until all the permits were granted and it became viable to sell. The market had risen and she made a fine profit. Living well is the best revenge . . .

Gianfranco the Wanker

Gianfranco was tall, dark, handsome and suave as a guava. Suzie met him around the pool at her holiday apartment. He charmed her with romantic walks along the beach, dreamy dinners under the stars, bouquets of heady scented jasmine and so much hot abandoned sex she could barely walk unaided to the Departure Gate. She flew home on the wings of love and kept the memories alive by phone and fax. She suggested visiting him in Rome for the weekend. He agreed, told her to pay her fare, but he would pay everything once she arrived. She bought an entire new wardrobe, had her hair cut and coloured and told everyone who would listen about her luscious Latin lover. He was cool at the airport and talked little on their way back to his apartment. He left her alone that first evening saying he had to 'work late'. His fridge was all but empty. On his return, he flopped down on the bed where he stayed for the entire weekend in an old vest and grubby Y-fronts watching the Sports Channel while fondling himself. When he fell asleep, she switched the TV off. He snorted loudly and switched it on again. He showed no interest in her nor in the contents of her expensive lingerie. He made one fumbling attempt at *amore* but gave up when Lazio equalised with F.C. Firenze. She noticed he had peasant's feet. At the end of the weekend, he took her to the airport and for the benefit of the general public, squeezed both her breasts possessively and mockingly smacked her buttocks.

Moral. Holiday romances are like bikinis: the briefer the better and remember they perish when you get them home.

The Bouncing Czech

'Would you like to become my third ex-wife?' Not bad as chat-up lines go and so Elaine agreed to have dinner with the portly, hirsute, academic bohemian with the strange-sounding name. His company promised to be more entertaining than the last few dates she'd had with the usual run of baggage-laden rejects and losers who pass for suitable men these days (pause to remove bitter herb from back of throat). His conversation was peppered with references to his youthful struggle against communism, his fascination for Roman pottery, his success as an amateur dramatist in the fringe theatres of Eastern Europe, and, as the booze took hold, his masculine prowess and bolshie boasts about what great lovers the Czechs are (the only czechs I have ever loved are the ones made out to cash). He certainly had a fabulous evening listening to himself talking about himself while sitting opposite an attractive companion apparently hanging on his every word. But when the bill arrived, to Elaine's surprise and indignation, he expected her to pay half. At a loss for the correct way to object, Elaine stumped up, notwithstanding the fact that he had invited her to dinner, ordered for both of them, selected and drunk most of the wine, all the while rejoicing in the sound of his own voice. On relating the story to her friends, she was met with a barrage of opinions all of which amounted to 'No Way You Pay'. On being asked for a second date, she agreed, planning a different tack for the solidarity of the sisterhood. The conversation was repetitive: more childhood, more politics, more pots, and more pseudo-intellectual ramblings liberally laced with attempts at hand-holding and increasingly suggestive propositions, all played out in a cheaper restaurant. His belief in his own attraction increased with his alcohol consumption, tempting Elaine to mutter: 'If you're so fabulous, why not go fuck yourself?' According to her plan, she took a lengthy visit to the Ladies' Room around bill bringing time. On her return, there it sat, still unpaid, in its little straw basket. The wine bottle was, once again, empty. He had ordered a brandy, which had been added to the total.

'Yours comes to . . .' he began, and then Elaine told him exactly what hers came to:

For listening to you gassing on about your tragic childhood: No Charge
For feigning fascination while losing the will to live: No Charge
For averting my gaze when you dropped mashed swede into your lap: No Charge
For having my personal space invaded by an unkempt beard with wandering hands and designs on my person and my purse: No Charge

Needless to say, he was not amused. He argued that if women wanted to be emancipated feminists, they could not do it half-cocked, ergo: 'You vanna behave like a man, you gotta pay for your own dinner.' But we do not want to behave like men. We spend hours getting ready (anyone know any blokes who do that?), we arrive on time, freshly bathed, waxed, coiffed, dressed and made-up. We provide stimulating eye and arm candy and interject female frippery and/or womanly wisdom to their dull discourses whenever we are able to get a word in. We do not sit with our legs *oisgeshpreit,* scratching, belching and talking with our mouths full, nor do we lean back from the table in a slovenly slouch in order to accommodate our unsightly gut. When the streets are safe to walk alone, when the jobs and wages are commensurate with the work undertaken irrespective of gender, when we are not treated as vassals and vessels by our so-called 'partners', maybe then we can talk about equality. And paying for our own dinner . . .

'Darling, you're not supposed to call afterwards for at least two weeks . . .'

2
SEX MATES

Maggi Russell

I ain't looking to compete with you,
Beat or cheat or mistreat you,
Simplify you or classify you,
Deny, defy or crucify you.
All I really wanna do
Is baby, be friends with you.

(Bob Dylan)

Between men and women there is no friendship possible.
There is passion, enmity, worship, love, but no friendship.
(Oscar Wilde)

Whether you are hunting for your soulmate (and we all
know how long that can take), a commitment-phobic love-
cynic, or just looking for some part-time physical recreation,
there's quite a lot to be said for that old hippie concept of
'loving the one you're with'. At the very least, having sex
with people that you also happen to like is a lot more
sensible than having sex with strangers. But we have to
acknowledge right away that the very concept of sex with
mates is something of a contradiction. One of the weird
side-effects of sex (along with five o'clock shadow of the
nooni and the post-coital inability to say anything even
vaguely intelligent for at least two hours) is that people who
have sex together simply cannot be friends as well. Think

about it – friends are those indispensable people whom you ring: before dates, to share your attack of nerves; after dates, to share your attack of remorse; and even during dates, when you want to attack with something spiky. Friends pick you up when you're stranded in strange places, accept your calls at 4 a.m., and tell you bluntly when your hairstyle needs rethinking. None of these things can be done with people you are actually *schtupping.*

Sex demands a thorough coating of fantasy to make it tasteful. A bit like cod. You can never be wholly and completely honest with someone you have seen naked. There are things we must pretend not to have seen, and things we must pretend not to have known. Like nudists playing ping-pong. In sex, there are very strict rules of make-believe. Even animals know this. Lions fluff up their manes, and pretend to be helpfully grooming the backs of their females' necks. Peacocks parade campily in carnival costume, and distract with drama. Flamingos do a kind of fandango. And then, bingo! It's sex.

If the beloved is to remain magnetic, s/he must also remain paradoxical, and somehow inexplicable. We have already said that sex cannot be understood. It's a primeval force with a necessary built-in antagonism. It's certainly not *friendly.* So, if you don't want to remain celibate, but are not currently in love, how do you manage a sex life without monogamy or commitment, but with plenty of affection and respect? How, in other words, to have IT without feeling like a harlot?

Under the terms of engagement described in this book, when we refer to 'friends' we have sex with, we shall also be calling them boyfriends, who in our new millennial kind of meaning are nothing like the last century's *boyfriends,* but neither are they anything like girlfriends. Because they are also sex *fiends.* And, unlike girlfriends, they can absolutely never be told the truth. About anything. Ever. Tattoo that in

Braille on your inner arm, or pick it out in luminous stars on your bedroom ceiling, lest you forget. Also forget that tired old euphemism 'boyfriend' when used to mean monogamous, committed situations. Anything that serious needs a much more grown-up title. (Any suggestions? *Partner* and *mate* sound more like plumbers' assistants.) Here we are using the term 'boyfriend' to mean what it really ought to mean – people whose company you enjoy and want in your life like girlfriends, but because they're not permanent fixtures (although they may, over time, become real friends, albeit ones who probably would still like to shag you) and because they've got penises, they've got a different handle. Sex with a boyfriend fulfils a basic human need in times of scarcity, on a par with sharing chocolate ice cream and dating anecdotes with a girlfriend. Very pleasant, educational and good for the internal musculature (pelvic with him, diaphragmatic with her, *vis à vis* all that rapid quivering and hollering) but it doesn't mean you are necessarily going to want to do it again tomorrow, the next day, or for the rest of your life.

Sorry to get pedantically semantic, but we just can't stand words that don't fit, and are just coy leftovers from some 'Happy Days' yesteryear, when boys came calling at 7 p.m. bearing a corsage wrapped in cellophane. We also don't like euphemisms such as 'going out with', or 'seeing'. 'Dating' is better, because you do have to make a date, although without necessarily ever having another one. (Hookers use this phrase, as in 'Wanna date, mister?' and they are nothing if not realistic.) You may think this is all pointlessly academic. (And who am I to speak, being a person who actually gives over substantial mental energy to issues such as 'Why is pork such a versatile meat?' Ham, bacon, sausages, scratchings, pâté and meatballs all taste noticeably different, while lamb, a similarly fatty mammal, always tastes just like lamb, and is an abject failure as a sausage. Just be grateful you don't have to live inside my head – MR.)

Which comes down to one of those fiendish, fascinating, fundamental facts of life – something that even scientists with brains like planets, and spiritual leaders with auras like suns, agree upon. *Everything* in life is a paradox. Everything is two things at the same time. Matter and anti-matter both emerged from the big bang at once. When they met, they should've destroyed each other. Except, they didn't, and the universe evolved. Subatomic particles exist as matter and anti-matter simultaneously. It's all one big mind-bending paradox. Like the person you adore most is also the person you often hate most and want to watch die agonisingly of a mystery virus, while you look on with a triumphant, gloating, unwholesome expression from the foot of the bed, like Mrs Danvers, anti-matter incarnate. And those who give you the warmest, cosiest feeling round your heart (your children) are also those who revel in sticking bamboo shoots under your nails (with their smoking, shagging and truanting) and shrug off your shrieks of pain as they grow. Likewise, while sex is definitely the most pleasurable pastime on the planet (don't listen to those sad onanists who'd rather have a cup of tea or eat chocolate or watch Beckham bending) it is also undoubtedly the one that brings the biggest backwash of anguish in its wake. And the pleasure is commensurate to the amount of pain. Sex with people you might be in love with bears all the exquisite torment of being smeared with caviar and nibbled to death by fluffy kittens with sharpened teeth. (The Japanese, they of the delicate ways with bamboo, always an inventive and experimental race whether applying themselves to flower arranging or artful agony, undoubtedly tried this one, along with boiling other people in oil while making love, so as to *frisson* erotically to their death screams, and no doubt have even devised a way of death by origami – maybe folding you into a chicken like that poor woman in *Freaks*.)

Sex with friends is not nearly so passionate. But what it can provide is fantasy, and you can train your boyfriends to perform masterpieces of sexual charades. (Remember the Sundance Kid, breaking and entering, and Katherine Ross complying to his every whim at gunpoint? You could try this with your favourite Yardie. And Butch was up for being one of her boyfriends, too. 'I will not stay to see you die,' she cried dramatically, before sweeping out on them both. How many times have you longed to say *that* after your company has drained the cocktail cabinet?)

But Never Ever Have Sex With Your Best Friends!

This is an absolute fundamentalist, biblical law. Where your *real* male mates are concerned, wear a burka. If you are lucky enough to have a genuine male friend in your life who loves and supports you, even if he secretly would like to shag you but has the decency to keep quiet about it, never ever *ever* blow this beautiful friendship. He is your brother. Sleep with him and the whole deal will spiral into chaos, you can't go forward and you can't go back, and so you may very well implode. Yes, it's tempting – you think you can handle it. Trust me, neither of you can. One of you is bound to want to take it further, and will freak out the one who doesn't. Getting a friendship back on track after a *schtupp* is impossible. Unless you are both inhumanely cool, like futuristic cybernauts or something, sex can ruin a friendship faster than an unpaid loan.

Sex with friends in our simplest terms means sex with men you are not in love with, and aren't likely to be lifelong friends with either. You will never be giving him girlfriend advice, or going home to meet his mum. The two of you do not get emotional, except perhaps over football. You both know, but never actually say, that you are only enjoying each other while you are waiting to fall in love – with somebody else. In fact, anybody else, because you know, perhaps a little sadly, you are not suited for the long haul, for too many reasons, both subtle and prosaic. It would be much too crass to spell them out.

Both of us have had such boyfriendships that lasted years. We were genuinely fond of them, found them very attractive and greatly enjoyed the sex, but couldn't possibly have lived with them. Plus there was the slight hindrance that they both lived with other parties. And we don't intend to be monogamous with men we don't own. We have of course realised by now that we are on a kamikaze, suicide-bomber-type mission with this manuscript, as no one who reads this is ever going to want to date either of us ever again. Not any of those from the past, present or foreseeable future, until it thankfully goes out of print. But fuck 'em all. For Queen and Country, Goddess and Sisterhood, we must speak forth our truth, and go down in a blaze of glory before we bite the dust. (Thus spake Zara Thruster, pornstar of this parish.)

So here comes the thorny issue of sex with boyfriends who are other people's husbands. (More about this in The Mistress chapter.) We do have a rule about this, believe it or not, and here it is. This is not a matter for your conscience, so long as you do nothing to hurt or disrupt the life of his main squeeze. (I can hear the outraged roar of the collected studio audiences of *Kilroy* and *Trisha* – don't expect to see us promoting this book there.) People love to blame the other woman – the slut/tart/Whore of Babylon. But if she is a graceful woman, she will never call him at home, she will make sure he doesn't leave her bed too late, always check him for stray hairs and lingering perfume, and never try to seduce him away from his family. Sensible wives and mothers will turn a blind eye to you, and certainly never turn up on your doorstep wielding miniature nuclear armaments. To divorce him because of you would be absolutely tragic. Wives need to take the Continental approach, where extra-marital affairs are part of their *entente cordiale*. A man who both loves his wife and is fond of his mistress is a contented man. We know of which we speak, having been on both sides of this particular barbed-wire fence.

Why men can't be monogamous is hard for women to fathom, the equivalent of trying to work out why $e=mc^2$ – we don't know why it does (Einstein didn't really know why, either) *it just does*. Or how matter can be both a wave and a particle at the same time. How? *It just can.* These are accepted universal laws. So although we hate to hand it to them, male sexual incontinence may be a natural law, too. Many men choose to be faithful, but they admit it's a struggle, and a lot of mental infidelity goes on instead. Many men adore – nay, worship – their wives as goddesses, but still fancy a quick poke with the twinky down at Car Mart. And they will risk their marriages into the bargain. To understand it, we'd need to walk around with penises in our pants for a week, and experience how this mysterious appendage spontaneously rises and falls like waves throughout the day, in response to random female stimuli. (Another scientific fact, while we're blithely bandying them about: two objects attract each other in proportion to their mass and in inverse proportion to the distance between them. In other words, put a bloke with a sizeable proportion in grabbing distance of an attractive object, and they will soon become one perverse heaving mass.) Apparently (so we are reliably told) once a real boner is in place, natural law decrees it must reach its conclusion, or something called 'blue balls' results. After such unsavoury interludes, these men usually rush home to Her Indoors more in love than ever, their adoration now given a piquant chilli saucing of guilt.

Women, on the other hand, do seem to tend towards monogamy – and most definitely so when in love. In fact, when in love it seems a total travesty of all that is sacred to sleep with another man. We all know the tired old theory of this being because of needing to know the father of any offspring. But we also saw that documentary about cheeky, resourceful little birds that pass their eggs off on to newly acquainted and blissfully ignorant males of the species, who then obligingly dash about providing worms, while everyone else in the tree knows exactly who got to do the actual fertilising round the back of the nest. Father identity is not a sound theory. Increasingly these days, women dump the donor once they have the foetus in place. It's more to do with female *scheduling*, we think. A male (spider, bat, alligator, man) does not feel that there is much point to his existence unless he is pleasuring females (and sadly he may have a point). They are incapable of planning ahead, so tend to think each vagina may be their last. But women have got all sorts of other more important things to do. They like to know exactly when they're going to have sex so they can work it in to their timetables. If they're doing Roger at 10 after dinner on Friday, there's no need to do Phil on Wednesday at 6. And anyway, Wednesday has already been set aside for a facial and cleaning behind the fridge, and women do not like to deviate. Men can and do just drop everything any time for a shag – because all the self-important things they are usually doing, like pillaging the resources of the Third World, bombing civilians, inventing plastic bottles that can remember their shape after being crushed, and devising gadgets for dispensing sticky tape (though they still haven't mastered that one), don't actually need doing at all. Of course, when not in love, a woman may have as many lovers on a string (a clutch?) as any randy man, but, generally speaking, she tends not to bother. If she does have more than one on the go, it's usually for harmony and balance, i.e. if she's got one randy, irresponsible bad boy on her books, she's also going to need a sensible, reliable one to even everything out. No one wants a life that is out of wack. If she's got two bad boys she may need two good boys to keep the scales on an even kilter.

So, whether your boyfriends are confirmed bachelors, cohabitees or refugees, this is not really your concern. His conscience is his affair. If you do try to insinuate yourself too far into his life he will probably dump you. And quite right too.

Another paradox is that guilty parties are likely to make more devoted and consistent boyfriends than any of your confirmed bachelors. These can be a very dicey bunch of spanners indeed. Never married – or perhaps once, briefly – they guard their frozen hearts like Scott's Antarctic tomb. To protect against falling for a woman they always have several on the go, and display a ready coldness to keep you at bay, should you get too affectionate. They may ring you up at midnight for amusing chats instead of using a sex line, they may be wonderful cooks, have great apartments, all the latest techno gear, fascinating jobs, be huge fun, but they also make it clear when it's time for you to leave. Also, unlike the marrieds who have to come to your place, they prefer to date you on their own territory so they can maintain the control, both remote and hands on, as they have 100 channels – including porn. The irritations are contingent. They boast about all the fab celebrities they know, parties they've been to, holidays on yachts, etc., etc., and never invite you along to anything. This is because they are always hunting fresh flesh, and aren't going to take you anywhere where there might be hot new babes to add to their portfolios. If they are just too mean, pass them on, declaiming like Connie, Doris Day's best mate in *A Touch of Mink* (1962), 'You are a sneaky, crude, offensive man – I'm sure there are lots of other women in this town who'd appreciate those qualities.' While the perky Doris was offered a trip to Bermuda and a mink coat in return for her favours, today, unfortunately, it's more likely to be Viagra and a porn video. *C'est la vie*. (N.B. This film also stars the divine Cary Grant, and I do think that if you ever find yourself in a situation where you are at a loss for what to say, or how to behave, just ask yourself what he would do, and do that.)

Paradoxically, these men are actually the loneliest individuals on earth, because they can never ever afford to feel real love. This is too risky for them. So the sweeter he's been, expect the backlash to follow at once. One friend tells us that after her current squeeze has entertained her to a particularly delightful and colourful evening (music, dancing, strip poker, interesting forfeits – a whole Bollywood extravaganza of a date) she knows she won't hear from him again for at least three weeks. A mediocre date and we're all guaranteed a midweek call, just to check we're still alive. Worse, they may want to tell you about their sexual exploits with other women. Disabuse them of this. Unless you are into a perverse Marquise de Merteuil and Vicomte de Valmont kind of trip (or dating John Malkovitch), you don't really want to be *that* sophisticated, do you? You do not want to know. Do they want to hear how you were shagged senseless yesterday by the cute guy from the garden centre? I rest my case. (We hope those chicks who wrote *The Rules* are reading this and having apoplexy.)

So how can you tell in which category to put a new man that you meet – one date, two dates, boyfriend or soulmate? If he's good company, generous, a good shag and fun, but emotionally weird, then he most definitely deserves to be a boyfriend. DO NOT FALL IN LOVE WITH HIM. Take a cautionary warning from the story of Simone de Beauvoir, an exemplary female in many ways, but who most ill-advisedly fell madly in love with Jean-Paul Sartre, and thought of him as her soulmate, while he delighted in regaling her with accounts of his many other conquests. He even insisted on taking her along on his dates, just for fun. Ditto Kenneth Tynan's long-suffering wife Kathleen, who had to put up with Ken's penchant for spanking sessions with some strange creature called Nicole. Steer well clear of *any* soulful, sophisticated man with zany specs or a newspaper column who strolls up claiming that 'to do is to be'. There are certain doings that most certainly should never be, or at least should never be recounted. If any men should ever have been regarded as 'just boyfriends', existentially speaking, it was them.

Remember, you are only doing this while waiting for your soulmate. It might have been that last boyfriend, if only he hadn't come home unexpectedly early from school in 1952, and caught mother with the plumber. But he did, and now he's emotionally darkened. But luckily for him, he has worked out a way to have all the *poonani* he can eat, and blame mummy for that, too. He has much too much invested in being fucked up to give it all up for you. So please DON'T TRY TO CHANGE HIM – thinking you could be the one. Our hearts bleed for all the obsessing that women do over some total bastard who has already broken the hearts of hundreds before you washed up on his shores. These men often do marry, eventually, but it will be a cold-blooded choice – someone young, attractive, and, later on, capable of being a good nurse. As the peerless Oscar W. explained, men only marry because they are tired. You are much too feisty, ballsy, demanding and exhausting for him. After dating you he probably lies on the sofa for 12 hours with a glassy expression. He knows he is your inferior. He doesn't want to be reminded of it every sodding day. So enjoy him as a boyfriend while you can.

This brings us to the question of your own boyfriend

casebook. (Like mental patients, you need to keep files on them all.) You are going to need a selection, a pick'n'mix – one for every occasion. A good hand might go like this:

- one of 28–35 (beautiful body, great stamina, always horny, you can mother him),
- one crazy muthafucka (see above) and
- one sensible chap your own age who adores you and can be taken to visit your aged mother.

Three is all any sensible girl can handle, and of course they'll have to be replenished regularly from the inexhaustible source of God's bounty as they disappear through natural wastage. Probably the young one will settle down and get married (though may still want to see you!), the crazy mutha' will piss you off so much that eventually you'll dump him (if you run into him at a swishy event with a woman on his arm he chose to take instead of you – that could definitely be curtains), and the sweet one will eventually dump *you* 'cause you are breaking his heart with all your run-around ways.

In those not infrequent intervals in history when humanity careered off the rails and embarked on one long insane party (La Belle Époque, The Renaissance) courtesans held sway over the social world, rather like movie stars and supermodels today. These *grandes horizontales* were economically independent, unmarried women, who chose their lovers from among royalty, politicians and artists, and managed to be the toast of the town at the same time as being scandalously immoral. They differed from mistresses in that they were not expected to remain attached and faithful to one man, but could have as many on the go as they liked. This was definitely sex with friends, only with extravagant gifts factored in as well. Famed for their elegance, style, intelligence and wit, they gave the best parties in their salons, and the best private entertainments in their boudoirs. Cora Pearl, at one of her soirées in the Paris of the Gay Nineties, served herself up as dessert, displayed naked on a dish and covered in swirls of chocolate and cream. Her guests set to work to lick every inch of her body clean. No wonder men worshipped these women, painted them and wrote novels about them, and often squandered their entire inheritances to keep them in chateaux and jewels.

Today, we no longer build up our fortunes from the estates of ruined paramours, but have had to learn to earn our own keep in more prosaic ways. Which is probably no bad thing. But although we may not be objects of scandal anymore, instead we seem to have lost a form of respect that our horizontal sisters unquestionably enjoyed. Courtesans were admired for flouting all the rules. Today, with no rules to flout, there is little *joie de vivre* to be had from immorality. And paying our own way somehow devalues the worth of our female *jouissance*. Men somehow seem to get more out of sex without commitment than women do. So, if he is getting his way, shouldn't he pay?

A very tricky issue this. If he always pays, he may feel he can call the shots. And then you may feel like a hooker. (Courtesans got paid, and still managed to call the tune, because they were exceedingly smart.) If he doesn't pay, then he may treat you like another bloke, as in 'It's your round, mate'. We would suggest you vary your approach according to his means. If he's broke, pay your way. If he's rich, encourage him to pay. If you're equally solvent, buy each other little gifts. At the end of the day, a man with any style at all will usually pay in restaurants, and you can repay him by making dinner in your home. Meanness is probably on a par with fungal infections of the fingernails as the greatest turn-off in men. In women, apparently, it's gold-digging. Even more reason why you need more than one boyfriend – one in each financial category. If the gorgeous one is the broke one, and the nice one is the rich one, so much the better – you've got it all going on. The crazy one will probably be larging it one minute and in prison the next, so be flexible.

The Ex Files

We must say something here about the thorny question of sex with an ex. Or rather, the complete invalidity of this as a workable concept. Back is one direction in which you should never go, particularly with the father of your children. (I confess, I lapsed once, and once only, and we only cuddled, honest. Number One Son, finding his drastically hungover parents in bed together the following day, replied to my anxious probing regarding the potential trauma, 'Don't worry, Mother, you desensitised me years ago'.) If you are on good terms, even flirtatious ones, this is the best of all possible worlds. Let them think the world of you, let them see you were too good for them, let them fantasise about having sex with you – even hold out the carrot that one day you just might – but in reality, never ever do it. For that would be a total disaster – putting Pearl Harbor in the category of a minor mistake. Two minutes into the post-coital vacuum, horror and regret will rush in, as you remember every single reason why you originally broke up with him. Make your excuses and leave immediately, preferably for a long sojourn overseas.

Don't doubt yourself and the choices you have made. Your life means whatever you want it to mean, and others will always take you as you take yourself. Do it all with consummate style, and remember, je n' regrette rien. When the four horseman of the apocalypse come cantering up to your front door on Judgement Day, alongside War, Famine, Pestilence and Plague, there will be Regret, on a little piebald pony. Give them all short shrift, and send them on their way.

Does this all sound horribly heartless and bitchy? Are you saying 'A pox on your paradox'? Well here it comes again. You really do have to be a generous, loving and humorous woman to conduct this kind of life successfully. That's because you won't be using anybody, changing anybody, lying to anybody, stealing from anybody or judging anybody. (And, as Oscar said, a woman who moralises is invariably plain.) You will need patience, tolerance, grace, acceptance and an unshakeable sense of the ridiculous to handle the constant disappointments when dates go wrong or are cancelled, leaving you longing for real love. Just see it as part of your development from chick to chic. All we are saying is that this is an option while you are waiting for your soulmate, and it's much more honest and independent than dating some poor sucker who thinks you're into the relationship as much as he is – only for you to dump him when someone better comes along. Men get seriously damaged and embittered by this sort of treatment, and the next poor woman who loves him will bear the brunt. This is something we really hate to see – women who think it's okay to manipulate men because they're afraid to be alone. This is a colder, meaner way to conduct your life than to honestly have a few lovers, all of whom you are genuinely warm, kind and affectionate to. A real friend, in other words. Except with sex. And with that, our old adversary, paradox, comes charging up on horseback, once again.

'I usually have biscuits, but buns will do just fine . . .'

3

An Unsuitable Boy

Wendy Salisbury

. . . I'm feeling quite insane and young again
and all because I'm mad about the boy . . .

(Noël Coward)

We all know about the Sugar Daddy scenario – older man
with younger woman, much heralded by other gents in a
whey-hey kind of way. It's what bored marrieds or newly-
single middle-aged men aspire to when they've grown tired
of the woman they chose in their twenties as a life partner.
However, the reverse of this arrangement – older women
with younger men – is now the zeitgeist of social
acceptability, with sexually empowered and financially
independent women of a certain age living happily (n)ever
after with some very juicy pieces of what was once
considered forbidden fruit. This current trend simply
reflects one of the many choices now available to all of us.
On the horizontal front (back or side) the arrangement
works extremely well. Each has something the other wants
and the exchange is effected in the most satisfactory way –
you scratch my back, I'll do whatever you like to yours. The
most common imbalance with this type of hook-up is the
financial one and it is not unusual for the older woman to
pay for the privilege and pleasure of consorting and
cavorting with a younger man. Norma Desmond in *Sunset
Boulevard*, Mrs Stone in *The Roman Spring of . . .* and many a

lady with a full wallet and an empty bed are only too happy to treat the kid to a new wardrobe, a fast car, and a gold-engraved cigarette case with matching lighter, as long as he devotes himself entirely to her. Although celebrities may flaunt their junior arm candy with the same élan as the latest designer handbag, sophisticated ladies everywhere are fully aware that for the younger man, older women are definitely IN, and I'm not referring to the crinkly from Croydon with her young Masai warrior. A recent survey among men in their twenties revealed that most of them would rather date Anna Ford or Francesca Annis (both fifty-eight!) than any of the Spice Girls. So if you want to stay fit and hold on to your youth, find yourself a fit youth to hold on to. This may sound easier said than done, but later I will reveal how and where to find them.

Call me misguided but with no regrets, I (WS) have loved and lived with more than my fair share of younger men. It began on a skiing holiday with a major come-on from a very cute guy in the next door apartment. I was forty-two and I gauged him to be about twenty-seven (naughty but nice . . .). I had no lascivious intentions whatsoever but *he* did, which I discovered to my benefit after a rather abandoned and inebriated celebration of New Year's Eve when we left the party early and slithered giggling down the slippery slope to celebrate in our own particular way. When the subject of age inevitably came up, he endearingly mentioned that he was 'nearly twenty'. I took a tumble in more ways than one and from then on I was hooked, because like Pringles, once you've popped, it's hard to stop. The liaison has continued on and off ever since. We come together at home and abroad with a familiarity and comfort borne of knowing that neither of us expects anything more from the other than sex for the sheer enjoyment of it.

A younger man is like a rainbow that arcs across the darkening sky of your later life. With him, the highs are so high that having reached them, you just never want to come down. The flattering fact that he wants to play with *you* as opposed to children his own age, will make you eschew sense and sensibility for sex and sensuality. The feelings engendered are much stronger than those experienced with your peers when you were also young. We took so much for granted then and didn't necessarily appreciate the physical attributes of our own or our boyfriends' bodies. If anything, it was considered racy to go out with an older man. I went out with a man of twenty-five when I was sixteen and that made me feel incredibly superior and worldly-wise. My dad soon put a stop to it, especially as said chap was not only 'older', but also on the stage (West End, natch). But when you are approached by a junior in later life, it is incredibly gratifying and rather wild. Emotionally, however, you may as well run away and join a circus, for one minute you're a trapeze artist in a sequinned basque unicycling along on a high wire, the next you may be face down in the dust, your make-up streaked with tears while an elephant stomps on your heart. As far as getting a buzz goes, being seduced by a younger man is like plugging yourself into The National Grid. It makes your hair (what's left of it after the full Brazilian) stand on end, your heart pound, your pulse race, your bones melt and your organs pulsate with the sheer joyful lust of it. Just like being in love – ONLY DON'T, for that way madness lies. If you fancy trying this option for yourself, here are some of the pitfalls you should be aware of.

First off, you must adjust your mindset to the fact that these encounters will be brief. Young men are unreliable and can be cavalier with your timetable, and although they sport trendy watches that bleep at inopportune moments, they rarely use them to check the time. Meetings will be infrequent and you may get dumped at the last minute if the Man. United v. Real Madrid match is live on TV. If you're cooking for him, buy food with the longest Use By date. It'll keep in case of cancellation and you can feed it to your children, who *will* turn up even when the Boy Wonder doesn't. And don't waste money on the Hand-reared Freshwater Scottish Border Organic Salmon because you might end up ripping it apart with your bare hands and stuffing it through his letterbox. Although you will feel like a fantasy-fuelled teenager on the way in, you may feel like a floundering old fool on the way out, what with your fridge full of lager, your drawers full of pole dancers' lingerie, your bedside cabinet full of flavoured condoms and your bathroom cabinet heaving with Edible Honey Massage Oil and Chocolate Body Paint (which you have to remember to hide in case your children ever come round in search of an aspirin). So, with all this in mind, why even go there? Because when it happens, it's fucking gorgeous, that's why. And easy. Like giving candy to a baby. Coming from the Carpe Diem School of Irrational Behaviour and a great believer in that old adage, 'You're a long time dead,' I would let no opportunity pass me by no matter how unsuitable the suitor. Lovers come and lovers go, but memories (Alzheimer's permitting) last forever. So get out there and make some memories.

The Joy of a Toy Boy

Age does not protect you from love.
But love, to some extent protects you from age.
(Jeanne Moreau)

The expression 'toy boy' is not my favourite one but it is an apt description nevertheless. A 'toy' is something you play with: you unwrap it, examine it, turn it over and under, check all its moving parts, open and close it, see how long it can keep going for, discard it, pick it up again and generally take pleasure in it. 'Boy' because although fundamentally all men are boys, these little treasures have birth certificates and bodies to prove it: satin-smooth skin, surfboard-flat stomachs, pumped-up pecs, tight, taut glutes, hair in all the right places (as opposed to flowering out of their noses and ears), they are a feast for all five senses. (Try to get a photo to show your friends.) To drink from the fountain of youth is the most ambrosial elixir you could ever imbibe, fulfilling the parts of you no other beverage can reach. You must live in these moments for they will be transient, so put the future on hold, forget the past and bring to the present all the wealth of (s)experience and (s)expertise you have gleaned along the way. You may find yourself acting far more wanton than with lovers your own age or older. You are in it to sin it and this is not the time to be coy or virginal. He's had enough of all that teenage fumbling by the time he's reached twenty-five and he is with you because he is turned on by your maturity. He will revel in your womanly attributes and devour you with relish and delight, oblivious to the fact that said attributes may be heading south for the winter. This is a good time for you to forget that too. It bears little importance. Just keep doing the pelvic floor exercises. When lying horizontal, find poses that prop up the droopy bits and only go on top in a total blackout. Just as much as young men are some women's fantasy, so older women are theirs, and we all know about fantasies – best kept in the head under cover of darkness.

Where to Find Them

I can dance with you honey,
If you think it's funny,
Does your mother know that you're out?

(*Andersson/Ulvaeus*)

You are going to have to be a tad provocative and predatory here, while remembering to behave like a lady at all times in public places. Retaining a high level of personal maintenance and always looking your best 'just in case' can be a bit of a chore, but I believe one should do this anyway whether you are going to The Oscars or pushing a trolley round Tesco. You are more likely to meet Master Right doing the latter, so no baggy tracky bottoms, sweat-stained T-shirts or tea-stained sweatshirts please. Next, get a good mirror and take a long, cold, hard look at yourself. If you cannot find fault, close this book and go straight to Moorfields Eye Hospital. In a world where artificial assistance of every kind is just a chemist shop away (bigger branches of Boots now do Botox), developing and enhancing your best points with the aid of cosmetics, chemicals and collagen is the obvious option. Most of you are dealing with this already, and if you're not you should be. If necessary, treat your face, skin and hair to a mammoth make-over and be thankful that the ladies Lauder and Rubinstein were born before you. It's all out there, choose it, buy it, use it. Once you have the extra confidence gained from knowing you are looking your best, you will feel ready to tackle what lies ahead.

The Subtle Art of Seduction

Women have to learn that nobody gives you power. You just take it.

(Roseanne Barr)

Be aware in every aspect of your daily life of who is around you. Although I believe in instant chemistry, this can be built upon with available men you already know and like by sending out the right vibes. So firstly, make eye contact. When you talk to a younger man, whether you fancy him or not, look at him directly with a definite maybe in your eyes, using the wiles bestowed upon you at birth by the Fairy Goddess of Flirting. When it comes to seduction, most men are shallow, vacuous creatures much prone to flattery and the right kind of come-on. Even if you don't fancy him, use him as target practice. I'm not suggesting you blow the pizza delivery boy (really, Samantha!) but at least you will get an immediate reaction. It's instantaneous and unmistakeable. You'll enjoy the power surge that you generated when you see the erection in his eyes. And you don't have to be a classical beauty – Edwina will attest to that. If you don't currently know or fancy any likely lads, here are some suggestions as to where to meet them.

Late-night supermarkets: Do your food shopping in the evening and check out the bachelors buying TV dinners. If you like the look of one, ask him to reach something from a high shelf for you (damsels in distress will always be in vogue, no matter what the ladette/chick literati say). You never know, a conversation may ensue but if it doesn't, just put the tin of Chunky Celery Bites in Brine back discreetly on a lower shelf and move swiftly on.

Colleges and classes: Become a mature student and enrol in a course likely to attract youthful males. At best, you may hook yourself a lover, at worst you will gain a Diploma in the art of Motorcycle Maintenance with which to impress your son and his friends.

Sons' and daughters' friends: These are theoretically a no-go area, although it has been known . . . Your sons' mates are unlikely to view you in any other way than as 'Kevin's mum who makes a mean hamburger', but once you've finished titivating yourself and they've finished puberty, the balance alters. One day in walks a six-foot-two-inch testosterone factory who notices that you are 'Kevin's mum with the great legs and fabulous tits (who still makes a mean hamburger)'. If this goes the way it might, *for God's sake*, don't tell Kevin.

Daughters' boyfriends are another matter. The last thing you ever want to do is to alienate your little girl, nor encroach on her territory while she is still trying to work out exactly where that is. Think back to your own teenage years and how mortifying it would have been if your own mother had hit on any of your boyfriends. To your daughter you must remain above reproach: be a friend, an adviser, a sounding board, an ironing board, a chopping board even, but never, ever a rival for a man's affections. She's got enough male/female stuff to deal with, as have you, with the weekend father. But despite your outwardly impeccable behaviour (he can't read your thoughts, can he?) the young stud's male instinct may have picked something up from you. After all, you have a lot more to offer than his female peers do. In you, all their plus points have mellowed and matured into one superior package complete with all the Es any man could possibly want: experience, emotion, electricity, energy and, ultimately, ecstatic euphoria. And so he pops in to visit when she's away at Uni. You have to take a grown-up stance on how to handle this. Irresistible though a liaison may seem, I don't advise it unless you can trust him implicitly not to brag about it later on. The Devil inside may lead you to that dark place and once in the water you may as well swim (oh, those tantalisingly warm waves lapping over your body . . .) but remember that your daughter is a woman too, with the same instincts and intuitions as you, and she may pick up some very uncomfortable vibes next time she's home for the hols. I was thrown into this situation when an ex-boyfriend of my daughter's found himself homeless and she suggested he move into her room in my flat while she was away on her gap year. I'd always thought he was cute and the very idea of having him live with me sparked off all sorts of wicked thoughts. It quickly became clear the feeling was mutual, which engendered an atmosphere so charged you could have powered Manhattan with it. Although he had another girlfriend, we used to leave each other little notes and long, lascivious looks would pass between us whenever our paths crossed up and down the corridor at bedtime. We'd say 'goodnight' very correctly as we closed our respective doors, and I would then lie there in a state of high arousal waiting for him to pluck up the courage to creep into my room and slide in beside me. I couldn't bring myself to overtly seduce him, but the fantasy kept me going for many months . . . eventually, as is often the case, the fantasy proved far better than the reality!

The Personal Trainer/Tennis Coach: These chaps all fall into the same category. You will be one of many to them, another conquest, another notch on their bedpost. Although copious perspiring is not usually a turn-on, there is a certain carnal attraction between two people whose endorphins have just been stimulated. He won't need much encouragement and it will probably lead to nothing more than a sweaty coupling up against the lockers, not exactly good for your self-esteem but if all you're interested in is getting laid standing up, then go for it. My girlfriend, Emma G., found the distraction of admiring her coach's bulging biceps was hindering her tennis game. She spent more time watching his bouncing balls than the one he was lobbing to her over the net. She persuaded her old man to build a grass court in their massive garden so she could have Rod round for private lessons. Mr G. never understood why the court appeared unused (little did he know) nor why she was always pink and flustered on Tuesdays and Fridays with no improvement whatsoever in her game.

Estate Agents: If you put your home on the market, a procession of booted and suited boy babes will pass through your portals. Leave thought-provoking reading matter by your bedside, scented candles in your bathroom, a sliver of silk and lace peeping out from beneath your pillow and they may take the bait. Make the appointments at the end of his day and once the viewing has ended, ask if he'll stay to discuss the size of his commission. Offer him a cup of coffee or a glass of wine. Steer the conversation any way you want: contrary to popular belief, estate agents are humans too. You can also arrange for him to take you round the neighbourhood viewing other properties. The more time you spend together, the less time you'll spend talking about property.

I know this all sounds incredibly far-fetched and unlikely, but I did meet my last serious relationship, a man 21 years my junior, in exactly this way, and I wasn't even trying. After four months of verbal intercourse focused on the rise and fall of the property market, he falteringly confessed one evening that he really fancied me. I fancied him too, but would never have said it first. We fell on each other with all the pent-up emotion and desire we'd been too self-conscious to confess and exchanged and completed the contract later that same night. He moved in with me shortly after and we lived happily together for six and a half years that were the most stable and tranquil of my life, which surprised everyone, most of all me. Sadly, it ran its course, and while he temporarily disproved many of my cynical theories, since his departure and for the sake of my sanity, cynicism prevails again.

If none of these methods works for you, just bide your time, wait, look and listen. A woman I know got chatting to a young cabbie stuck alongside her in a traffic jam and arranged to meet him later for a drink. They had nothing in common except mutual lust, which was dealt with once a week at the Holiday Inn, Swiss Cottage until she became irritated with his opinions about politics and football. 'I'm a fuck not a fare!' she'd say to him, as she eased him into a place where dialogue was impossible.

People come in and out of your life when you least expect them, so stay alert to every possibility and go to The Opening of a Tin of Tuna if you think there will be fresh blood there.

Hormone Imbalance

Men and women reach their sexual peak at different times and there seems to be an illogical imbalance in society's perception of suitable partners. In general, the male is expected to be between two and seven years older than the female, for optimum success. The divorce rate proves that this is not working, so alternative arrangements have to be explored. There is a very real attraction between younger men and older women and it's not all Oedipal. The persona that you represent to a younger man is Everywoman, a Venusian composite of mother, lover, confidante, friend. He wants you to look after him, he wants to dominate you, he wants you to be available to him, he wants you to respect him for his achievements. For you there is a slightly incestuous slant to all this, being the paradox of 'mother versus lover'. A baby's first instinct is to search for the nipple, and to this flowing fount of food and gratification he will always return. This sets in motion maternal memories that did not occur when your suitably aged husband/ partner performed the same act. For if you close your eyes and stroke the dark, silky head of the boy-child at your breast, you will feel the sensual pull of a new-born babe mixed with the sexual appetite of a grown man . . . an ambiguous sensation if ever there was one.

Where Does it Go from the Bedroom?

Once you have found Mr T Boy, don't expect to go out much – that is not what this trip is all about. The attraction may be purely physical, in which case confine your time together to the pursuit of horizontal hedonism. The younger ones are usually broke and, more often than not, you will feel mismatched, no matter how hip you dress. You also take the risk of being inadvertently insulted by a gauche waiter. What could be more threatening to a romantic moment than hearing Luigi proclaim:

'Pizza Rusticana per lei, signor, and for your . . . aunt?'

Occasionally, they may offer to cook for you, which is a very sexy way to trash your kitchen. There will be all that reaching across each other while he weighs up the size of your melons and you'll be surprised how slippery an avocado can be once you've peeled its skin back. This is a really horny evening in and gives them back a little control over the relationship. You only need to provide the Häagen-Dazs, which can be consumed later every which way except with a spoon.

How Old Did You Say You Were?

Well, actually I didn't and I never will, although when planning the first holiday with my long-term younger partner, I decided I couldn't face playing 'hide the passport' for the entire trip and would have to fess up. Fuelled by Frascati, I plucked up courage and coyly asked him how old he thought I was. He naïvely guessed an age years younger than the actual one (bless). When I falteringly told him the truth, he shrugged his shoulders, smiled his sweet, slow smile, took my hand, placed it on the ever-increasing bulge in his jeans and leaned forward to kiss me. That was the greatest compliment I have ever received.

As life is not always that exceptional, you do have to be on your guard when doing and saying things that may date you, especially since presumably you have concealed your real age. I began a story once about being told off by my then boyfriend because I screamed at The Beatles in concert at the Finsbury Park Astoria (*c.* 1962) and then remembered that Toy had only just graduated from Cambridge with a double first in Maths. Whoops! Now I avoid the subject of my age altogether, but do occasionally lie about the ages of my children. Ten and twelve sounds so much better than twenty-eight and thirty-three, though what they are doing living in their own homes in the suburbs I haven't quite worked out yet. 'Tis a tangled web we weave . . .

Young chaps are eager to learn and will often listen enraptured to your stories, shaking their heads and muttering, 'You've done all that?' Depending on his education, he can even teach you a thing or two, so art galleries, museums and the Tate Modern are excellent (free) places to go where you can expound the merits of ancient-versus-modern and gaze into his eyes with unmasked adoration while he explains to you his interpretation of 'Pile of Poo with Purple Cement Mixer'. (Personally I think it's a metaphor for 'The World is Full of Shitty Gay Builders'.)

If the association is ongoing, you will at some point have to introduce him to your friends and family. The women will be green with envy and try to flirt in the gauche and giggly way other women have with their girlfriends' lovers, and the men will be green with envy and try to beat him at ballgames and boasting. Your mother will advocate pulling yourself together and ask you what on earth you've done with your hair, and your father will rustle the newspaper and pretend it's just not happening. His role has been totally usurped: he's made and paid for one (or two) weddings, suffered your mother's incessant bleating throughout your divorce(s) and is now stumped for questions since he's asked, 'Are your intentions honourable?' twice and been lied to both times. But what none of them can really cope with is the unmistakeable aura of raw sex that emanates from the pair of you wherever you go. You are so obviously getting it good, and they are so obviously not. Ha!

Without even trying, young men are able to please every part of you and dispense sexual largesse with ease just by being. The very fact of having a younger man at your side, in your home, in your shower and in your bed provides a *frisson* of expectation for the most jaded *amoureuse*, recharging your orgasmic batteries and confirming what you have always believed: you can still hack it, and no matter what your ex said during that last bitter argument, you are certainly not 'past it'. Here are some of the other pleasures to enjoy with the boy:

They are excellent eye-candy: I have sat in my kitchen and watched with anticipatory amusement while a very young Calvin-clad gentleman did my washing-up, secure in the absolute knowledge that once this well-hung Adonis with the rippling six-pack and the tight, firm buns had wrung out my squeegee-mop, he was going to lick my private plate clean and take me to the edge of Heaven and beyond.

They are excellent arm-candy: Just walking down the street with one incites the curious stares of strangers, which brings an extra spring to your step and a wicked grin to your face – for their dreams are your realities . . .

They can get away with looking scruffy: A young man with three days' stubble just looks hornier than usual, especially when you are both aware of what subtle movements he can make with his chin to extract that extra bit of bliss from you. An older man with three days' stubble just looks like he's lost the plot or is auditioning for the part of *Big Issue* salesman at the local Am Dram Society.

They wake adorable: Although by the very nature of their being male, they may snore (indulgence is required here) they are so cute and tousled when they awake, you cannot help but adore them. Everything is still in its rightful place, as opposed to being on the bedside table, dressing-table or the bathroom floor (teeth, hair, prosthetic limb, etc.) and no sooner have they stirred, than they're playing tents with your duvet. No matter how shattered and internally bruised you are from the previous night's shenanigans (don't you just love that pleasure-pain?) do avail yourself of this opportunity, for many will be the morning in the twilight of your years when you will wake alone and long for something long and stiff to reach out for. The remote control may be to hand to turn on the TV and video, but nothing will turn you on like he will.

What's in it for HIM?

Ask any man about his past and watch his eyes glaze over as he rekindles his memories of The Older Woman. Without exception, they have all had one and in many cases she was their first: the one to whom they gave their virginity willingly, an event that will always be remembered with fondness and nostalgia. Even if he was seventeen and she was twenty-one, this still qualifies, and when prompted to relate the story, they nod knowingly as they remember the life-altering moment when they first tasted the sweet richness of a real woman's ripe fruit. The Older Woman holds the key to the sexual universe, and once she unlocks the mystery within, the young man begins his carnal journey. No amount of peer-group sex can compete with a passionate adventure with a woman who not only knows her way around his body, but guides the eager student on his first erotic journey around hers. The high for him is bringing her to orgasm, and once he has achieved this, there will be no turning back. If she is adept and trains him well, he will graduate with honours and every woman he subsequently makes love to will have his first encounter to thank for his expertise and prowess. This training session is a two-way street. He wants to learn, she wants to teach, and between them they can indulge in many hours of exquisite exploration, the memories of which will remain with them until their dying day. Sexual chemistry is timeless and if the attraction is there, age is immaterial. The fusion of maturity and youth makes these encounters electric, each one bringing to the experience their own brand of passion. The man-child, at first awkward and timid, assumes a rather passive role, as the woman guides and controls him. Later, once he realises the effect his hands, lips and tongue have provoked, he becomes more self-assured and bolder and then the balance of power shifts and he assumes the role of leader. The woman, at first revelling in her position as instructor, is only too happy to give this up once their movements begin to merge and then she can lie back and enjoy the fruits of her teachings, praising herself for having made a competent man of an incompetent boy. Nothing is more pleasing for an older woman than to feel she has taken an innocent *ingénu* and turned him into a thoughtful, sensitive and romantic lover.

Once trained, he may grow so confident that he tries it on with other older women, often a superior at work. The thought that a high-earner in a powerful position can be reduced to a quivering love slave is a challenge in itself. The potential for controlling her swells his head and that swelling very quickly spreads. He wants to prove that, although she may be echelons above him in the company's hierarchy, he can match her in one particular area – between the sheets. In these days of social and sexual equality, the young man's role has been diluted and he is no longer sure how to play it with his female peers, who can work, play and drink him under the table, leaving him feeling insecure and uncertain. But with an older woman the understanding is that he is available to fulfil one particular purpose. The benefits for him are that he is not expected to organise, plan nor provide. She will make the arrangements and control the affair, all he has to do is turn up and turn on. She will not, unlike his female peers, try to turn him into the perfect man, experience has already taught her that there is no such thing. Nor will he be expected to spend a fortune wooing her. She is often pressed for time and will be quite happy to get straight down to business. Neither will she want him trailing round the shops with her on a Saturday afternoon like a normal girlfriend, as she will be too busy having a facial, manicure and highlights, or working in her home office preparing the sales pitch for the breakfast meeting first thing Monday morning.

Exceptions rule, OK?
Occasionally, the out-of-wack world we live in relaxes on its axis and one of these oddball relationships actually works out. There is no reason why it shouldn't, because the individuals involved are just that: individual. I've never known a younger man say that the age thing broke it up. If the relationship fails it's generally for the same reasons that make same-age unions falter – boredom, stress, breakdown in communications, work, money and family problems. Many a Hollywood diva (and lesser mortal) has made a perfectly successful marriage with a man young enough to be her on-screen son, so take heart and go with the flow. Don't assume it won't work, just be aware that it is less likely. On balance it has as much chance of survival as any other involvement, providing he doesn't mind skipping a generation and going straight to grandchildren.

The End of the Affair

> *You have to learn to leave the table when love's no longer being served.*
>
> (Charles Aznavour)

The Older Woman is a complete yet complex creature, matured and developed both mentally and physically, yet still vulnerable in matters of the heart. Our insecurities lie in the loss of our physical firmness, as we are forever having it rammed down our throats by the media that youth is the most desirable of all human qualities. Any man with a grain of a brain will realise that this is hogwash. We may have a fuller belly and more wobbly thighs but we exude the style, grace, confidence and sexuality that still lies dormant in our younger sisters. We manage our lives, our homes, our businesses, and our families, and this particular brand of authority can be a powerful aphrodisiac. But, the nature of the beast is to graze at the abundant watering-hole and, having grazed, move on to pastures new. This is when you will need every ounce of philosophy you have ever learned to get you through, a kind of womanosophy. If you can manage all the other aspects of your life, you are going to have to manage this. Because the sad truth is that the autumn-spring relationship rarely lasts. He will move on and, when he does, it doesn't matter whether you are sixteen or sixty, a broken heart is a broken heart. This one is a multiple loss, a bereavement plus empty-nest-syndrome all rolled into one. It compounds your loneliness, for when he goes, he not only takes with him the youth he returned to you, but also the joy, freedom and optimism he brought to the relationship.

It is impossible for me to tell you not to form attachments, because if someone makes you feel as exceptional as a young man does, it is natural for you to want this feeling to last forever. The brutal truth is: you've had your life, he's just beginning his. For you, the affair represented a last-ditch attempt to recapture your former glory and allowed you to behave in a refreshingly immature way, which you probably did not enjoy half as much when you actually were immature. For a while there, you could kid yourself that he and you were equal. Horizontally, you surely were, and no-one can take that away from you. He completed you in the most important area of your being and made you feel like a goddess glowing with the thrill of anticipation every time you had a date. These were emotions you never expected to experience again, so jaded had you become with your bad marriages, worse divorces, house moves, money worries and children coming and going. The gift of a younger man in your later years is not to be underestimated and you must tell yourself that what you gained in those fleeting moments were the sincerest form of flattery, for he hugged and kissed your very soul, enriching your life beyond imagination. To have your mind and your body seduced and adored in that particular way is a bonus and you must cherish the memories and thank God that you were blessed with this fabulous experience. And then you must love him enough to let him go . . .

Suzi was forty-one when she met Paul, twenty-eight. She was divorced, bright and stylish, an interior designer who had just completed a scheme for a boutique hotel that was to be photographed for an international magazine. Paul, the photographer, arrived with all his paraphernalia, dressed in scruffy jeans, biker's boots and a well-worn leather jacket, with stubble on his chin and grease under his fingernails, emitting an animal odour of pheromones and perspiration. He dropped his gear along with his aitches all over the bedroom floor. Suzi, a walking advert for the designer label, with a Belgravia accent and attitude to match, looked him up and down and wrinkled her nose in objection.

Despite this, a teasing voice inside her head whispered: 'Have him washed and brought to my tent.' They got off to an angry start as he had left muddy footprints all over the écru carpet in the Monaco Suite. He did not take kindly to being told off by this up-jumped posh bird and reckoned she needed a good seeing-to to shut her up. Whatever Suzi suggested, Paul disparaged. She wanted the drapes open, he required them closed, she suggested the bed be made up, he preferred it slept in. She arranged the towels in neat piles, he tossed them over the bath and sink. Annoyingly, when the photographs came out, he was proved right. She grudgingly admired his talent and began to employ him on all her shoots. He did his job creatively and tried to keep out of her way. On the day of the Interior Designer of the Year Awards for which she had been nominated, she was dumped by her boyfriend. Paul overheard the conversation, registered her fury and subsequent tears and casually tossed: 'Want me to take you?' in her direction. She looked at him and remarked patronisingly: 'It's black tie, for God's sake!' 'I'll pick you up at 7.' he replied. When she opened her front door, resplendent in Valentino, there stood before her the most gorgeous, handsome and aromatic partner she could ever have wished for. The evening was a triumph, and although Suzi did not get the Award, she certainly got her reward. On arriving home, a gallant Paul carried her over the threshold and took her straight to bed. The combination of the bit of rough with the uptown girl was electric. The next day, at her suggestion, he went home, collected his gear and moved in. Twin girls and a jointly-flourishing career later, they are a happy, confident, well-adjusted couple who have met somewhere in the middle of their different backgrounds, disproving the theory that you should stick to your own type. All things are possible – you just have to be open to them.

'I can't believe it! He even likes shopping for shoes . . .'

4
Soulmates

Maggi Russell

The one guardian of life is love, but to be loved, you must love.

(*Marsilio Ficino*)

Perhaps the most perplexing of all the modern mysteries that imbue the mid-life dating scene with the flavour of an overwrought Wagnerian Ring Cycle ('WHY doesn't he ring?' to 'Thank God, he rang!' and round the circle again) is the notion of The Soulmate. Or maybe it's an unsolved crime: who killed the concept? And where did they bury the corpse? To cut straight to the chase: do you believe in them or not? And if you do, do you have any faith at all that one day you will finally find yours? Eve undoubtedly had one in Adam, but cynics might say that's because there were no other distractions, and neither of them had very far to look. These days, with six billion people to sort through, it's more like searching for a needle in a rehab clinic, a gentleman in the Slug and Lettuce (city traders – 'nuff said) or a spiritual soul in a lap-dancing lounge. It's truly Mission Impossible. It would undoubtedly save us all a great deal of disappointment and wasted energy if we gave up on the entire soulmate concept altogether.

And yet – where would each sex be without the other? And if we are all meant to be together, why not for each of us a special lover? The original earth goddess had her male consort, and every subsequent female deity has had her 'significant other'. The male and female principles, being two halves of one whole – sun and moon, day and night, sky and sea, yin and yang, He and She – surely can't mean She and Dozy, Porky, Beaky, Mick and Titch? Today, it seems, we really do relate more to Circe, that lonely castaway – only in reverse – trying to turn swine into men.

Giving up on the fantasy seems the most sensible option, but whatever else we may claim in deep, dark moments of despondency, usually on the phone to a sister of mercy, in the aftermath of yet another unspeakable date with some chat-room charlatan, we all really do seem to nurture a little flame of hope in our hearts. It may be spluttering and smoky, it may be all but extinguished, yet still some little inner elf tends it and keeps it going, like the Olympic flame, only much more pathetic. Yes, we all really do yearn for that special someone with whom to negotiate life's highways and byways, someone caring, someone humorous, someone *safe*. And often it is the most cynical among us, the very ones who scoff the most convincingly, who harbour the hearts that hunger most.

Increasingly, disenchanted women everywhere are saying they've finally given up all hope. However, probe a little further, or ply them with a few more glasses of wine, and they will often admit that this is still, secretly, what they really really want. (This surely must be the esoteric translation of that curious 'Zigga Zig Ah' of the Spice Girls' anthem – the love that dare not speak its name?)

Men would admit to soulmate fantasies too, if only they were in the habit of admitting to *anything* vaguely emotional. Number One Son (to whom I – MR – constantly refer for evidence of the pure, innate male psyche, before it gets fucked up) who is sweet sixteen, and not yet embarked on sex's stormy seas, sees an exclusive ticket for two as the only way to cruise. Because his heart has not yet been sunk,

Soulmates

harpooned by some mean little minx, his boat is still afloat. This is undoubtedly going to get pulped on the rocks, but we must forgive them for they know not what they do (having done it, in my time, to several poor suckers myself).

So, if we all really want one, and it seems to be the most natural, preordained way for Things To Be, why is it so damned hard to find one? What is the insurmountable obstacle that stands between you and him? Would you know him if you saw him? Has he already been and gone? Was that him sitting next to you on the bus yesterday? Did you turn him down when you were fifteen? Was he on the Up escalator as you were going Down? Do we each have only one possible soul match on the planet? And if so, does he live in Abu Dhabi or Arizona – places you are never going to go? Has he, perhaps, already been run over by a truck? Gone to the other side and can only communicate with you through a medium? Become a transexual because you didn't get to him in time? Retired to a Tibetan monastery fed up with waiting? Is life really that arbitrary and cruel?

This is crazy talk – the ramblings of women whose minds are addled from so much waiting – like women in doctors' surgeries, who arrive with a minor rash, and end up becoming mentally ill, demanding prozac and valium after so much delay. The repeated dashing of hope every time the next name called out isn't theirs, and suffering in indignant silence as some bitch who arrives late swans straight in, while the ladies-in-waiting cross and uncross their legs and sigh, with nothing to distract them but dog-eared magazines infested with germs, both mental and physical.

Let us now set out our agenda, perhaps on a tablet of stone. WE REALLY DO WANT SOULMATES – call it out to the universe loud and clear, then move on swiftly to Item Number Two: How do we find them?

We need to digress a bit here, I'm afraid, before we get to the really useful advice about setting out on The Hunt. We need to define exactly what a 'soulmate' is. Having trawled through most of the available literature on this, I have only come across one definition that rings true. Unfortunately, it's not the same as people who've just stayed together for thirty years, through thick and thin. These can be some of the unhappiest couples imaginable – people who are just afraid to leave. Or, as can often be observed, one half of the couple yearns and sacrifices him or herself in imaginary soulmating, while the other uses this devotion simply to exercise control. Of course, there are soulmated long-term couples, but these are quite rare, and usually only the nicest, most deserving people, genetically predisposed towards mutuality, and able, when required, to put their partner's needs before their own. Nor is a soulmate the person you are most infatuated with. This is often just a heady cocktail of fantasy and sex. You project on to the chosen one all your inner dreams of perfection, which are then crushed when he turns out to be an ordinary mortal with corny phobias and irritable bowels. You're *very* lucky if he is the father of your children – often he is not. You probably chose him because of a series of events that took place simultaneously: your eggs cried out, you looked around, and there he was with the best-looking genes. I personally regret nothing in my choice of Baby Father: he is handsome, charismatic, interesting and wacky. But he is not my soulmate. He does not bring out my best self – and that is putting it mildly. Instead of my Lionheart Self, he brings out my whining, irritable, Chickenshit Self. Somehow, with the best will in the world, we make each other feel shitty. It's a class thing, he says, and he may well be right.

It took the genius of Carl Gustav Jung to say the most sensible thing I've ever heard about soulmates. He called them the *anima* and *animus*. Of course, Carl's take on this is much deeper and more profound than my cut-price, nutshell version, but this is all we've got room for here, so let's be brisk. Basically, he maintained that we all have a self within us, an archetype, that is of the opposite sex, and resides within the unconscious, far away from everyday awareness. The person that you meet who most closely represents your male, *animus* self, *that* is your soulmate. This happens because you project on to them your own repressed masculine self. It follows on logically then, that you can't know your soulmate until you fully know yourself, and all the people who inhabit you. We mature types are at a distinct advantage here. In fact, it has been argued that you *have to be middle-aged before you can find your soulmate.* That is because it takes that long to find out just who all the people inside you are. This is an encouraging idea, and I intend to stick with it. I hope I can convince you of this too, because it represents a major breakthrough in our investigations. The universal psyche is helping the soulmate squad with their enquiries.

First of all then, try to find out exactly what your male self is like. This is probably a mixture of the qualities you most admire in men, and those that compensate for your own limitations. Is George Clooney really the embodiment of your *animus*? Methinks not. It may more likely be George Castanza (*Seinfeld* fans will know what I'm saying). When the egg that is you was originally fertilised, there was a brief period while The Unknowable Force prevaricated over whether to make you male or female. When the female genes won the upper hand, the male genes didn't just slink away, tails tucked under. They are still there, hidden inside you, plotting insurgency. Supposing it had gone the other way for them? Supposing you had been born with a penis? What would you be like?

Interestingly, some women can easily reply to this, others are completely flummoxed. To illuminate, let me share with you my own curious tale. I didn't really learn how to be a girl until I was about nine. Before that I was a noisy, bossy, extrovert tomboy. A proto-punk. I loved penknives and chucking stones. I sat with my legs apart. I tortured insects. I called myself David, after the one that slew Goliath and became a King. I identified with Bronco Lane, and Paul Newman as *Hud*. I was Ozzy Osbourne in the making.

Culture soon beat this out of me. I learnt that instead of *being* a swashbuckling boy, my only option was to *date* a swashbuckling boy. To do this, I had to become a girl. So I did. Overnight, I ceased growing taller, and put all those growth hormones into developing huge breasts. I grew my hair, which, with a little chemical help, turned a glamorous shade of red. My freckles disappeared, my bum grew like Kenny Everett doing Rod Stewart. I started to date any beatniky, rock 'n' roll bloke I could find. It was never the same, they were never as heroic as I. My true *animus* now only visits me in dreams. But interestingly, people often tell me, unprompted, that they can see the rock star *manquée* in me. That, or the Artful Dodger (my alter-*animus*). Not a pretty female rocker, like Britney or Madonna, or even a fascinating androgynous one, like Patti Smith, but an over-the-top male one from the 1960s, like Robert Plant. Even though these days I dress in tasteful separates from Marks and Sparks, never, ever sing in public and my dancing style is timid, they can still imagine me with tossing hair, straddling legs, leather and chains. Somehow leaking through, like an ancient stain, is the guy I might have been. I content myself now with making over Number One Son, urging him on to a career in rock guitar, dressing him in black leather and offering to get his body parts pierced, much to his ongoing disgust.

I know intimately, therefore, what my soulmate is like. He is a musician, or some kind of philosopher, but not an actor. And definitely not a writer. He is very, very funny. He is wildly imaginative. He is good at making things, particularly out of wood. He has hair on his head, preferably dark, but little on his body. He has a well-developed feminine side, cries at sad movies, and likes discussing paint colours. He is kind-hearted, enjoys dressing up, and is into his grooming. He has strange phobias and weird hang-ups, and is frightened of crowds and red lipstick. He has sympathy with spiders, snakes and mice, and even displays tenderness towards slugs. He hates ALL sport. He is recklessly brave, and can be belligerent. He can also be sentimental, judgemental and embarrassing, and often says and does things that are extremely impolite. He hates snobs, and anything phoney. He doesn't have to be tall, rich or ambitious, and he doesn't even have to drive (I don't, finding traffic impossible, and also wouldn't if I was a man). I have been out with many variations of this man, many, many times over. I have recently broken up with two of him. That's because, unfortunately, he is also self-obsessed, self-delusional, insolvent, unemployable, jealous, unfaithful, excessive with alcohol and terminally unreliable. These are all qualities I know to be latent within myself, but, having grown up as a girl, I have worked hard, and (hopefully) successfully, at keeping in check. Males, it seems, never see the need to do this, and our culture encourages them not to. I cannot change my taste – it is one of the ingredients of my blood, and a component of my soul. It is me. All the nice steady men in the world with smart suits and sensible jobs could never wean me from him. I am doomed to scour mountain high and valley low, forest and plain, in search of my very own Peer Gynt. Poor cow, you say. What a price to pay. Yes, yes, I will pay, I will pay, if only he will come my way.

I humbly suggest you try this exercise for yourself, and I hope that, for your sake, your *animus* is nothing like mine. I pray he has a good job, a BMW and a Range Rover, shops at

Aquascutum, has a city flat and a place in the country, holidays in Barbados and is kind and generous to children and animals. But if *you're* not like that too, in some part of yourself, he is not for you. He's probably all peculiar and fucked-up just like mine. Take a look inside your soul. Follow the trail, smoke him out of his lair. Then you will be sure to recognise him when you see him out there, made flesh.

People do say that when you meet your soulmate/ *animus*, you get this instant weird feeling, like a brick has been dropped on your head – or a strange phenomenon is happening in your chest. Some inner door swings open, and something passes through. These chosen few always say they knew at once when they met 'The One'. And it had little to do with sex. With your soulmate/*animus*, every-thing he does, even the more questionable things, and the way he does them, are just right. It is just the way you would do them too, if you had a penis. He finds the same things funny. (That's a major clue.) He has the same priorities. He is probably of exactly the same level of physical attractive-ness as you. (George Clooney, bye bye now.) He is most likely on a similar level of worldly success. He has read the same books and likes the same food. You share unsettling coincidences in your personal histories. He smells divine. Chemically, he is ready to compound with you.

Are you getting an inner picture? Craving someone more handsome, more successful, more wealthy, more interest-ing, more popular than you is never going to work. (If you do manage to snag a man like this with cunning wiles, long-term happiness will not ensue.) Your soulmate is not going to improve you, he is not going to give you a life. He is only ever going to complement what you already are. If you and your inner *animus* are already intimate, and you are, right now, a fully integrated person, with a full spiritual life, arguably, you don't need a soulmate at all.

Sometimes, you even feel as if you *have* a penis. You are already complete. Perhaps you are even ready for androgyny, that next big stage in the life game, which may occur to you as a groovy option as you pass into old age (more of this in another chapter). But if you are still buying La Perla underwear, and still trying to decide whether you can get away with that thong for *just* one more year, you are still in the soulmate game, despite your superior psychic development. If you truly are this fabulous, but still want someone to love, your task may be quite complex. You may have to go for someone really quite seriously flawed, to balance you out. Interestingly, one sees this in action quite a lot. A fantastic, role-model of a woman, soulmating with a dickhead of a man. It should not be – and yet it seems to work, and she appears extremely happy and fulfilled. Don't interfere, she knows what she's doing. He's reflecting and expressing her shadow side – the dodgy, dickhead side of herself that has been so successfully repressed by her outward, superior, goddess persona.

While you're waiting to meet him in the flesh, like Frankenstein's monster waiting for his bride, you have plenty of work to do. Firstly, find out what is missing in your own psyche. Which bits of you do you neglect? Do you allow your masculine side any expression at all? If so, when? It doesn't mean you have to rush off to motorcycle maintenance classes, or take up welding. Your soulmate may not be any good at macho things either. If your *animus* is a gentle soul who loves books, then browsing bookshops may be where to find him. But if you have a repressed urge to sail the seven seas in an open boat, then it's probably at the sailing club where he awaits. It's no coincidence that many soulmates meet up while pursuing hobbies – because this is where we often express our secret fantasy *animus/anima* selves.

You've looked within, you've discovered your *animus*

and had a good look at him. You accept his flaws, and you think you'll know him when you see him. So, when you do finally meet, will it immediately be LOVE? Do we even know what we mean by this exhausted word? And has it always meant the same thing? Is a soulmate still a Tristan and Isolde, Anthony and Cleopatra, Romeo and Juliet kind of deal? Does it always have to end in tears?

Love is a word that should be taxed – you can't use it without paying. Until we can settle on some kind of realistic definition of this, we don't really know what we're talking about, do we? So what is this thing called 'Love'? Or what IS this thing called, love?

First of all, it seems to me that immature love goes hand in hand with yearning, and some people never grow out of this phase. The young are meant to yearn – it is an end in itself, and keeps them on track, developing strong enough egos to carve out their places in the world. The reward of wanting is not getting, but temporarily ceasing to want. When the young get something, it is seldom satisfying for very long. They start wanting something else almost straight away. Like having bought the black suede Russell and Bromley boots, you (OK, I) want the burgundy ones as well as soon as you (I) get home. And going back to part with yet another *insane* 250 quid, you think you will then possess the mother lode of bootyness – you will never need to fret about boots again. Into the wardrobe they go, where they rapidly coalesce into the dusty suede-layer, never to be objects of lust again. Warn your young: if they get their soulmates too soon in life, and cease to yearn, they may actually miss it. This manifests as boredom – so they split up, are riddled with regret forever, and never find true love again.

Grown-up love is only possible when a person can take complete responsibility for themselves and their actions towards others. An inner quality-controller guards the self against all temptation towards strategy and manipulation. It is a spontaneous willingness to do what is best for everyone involved. It is a real, not an ideal vision of other and self. It is the complete acceptance of another, the way they are, and a complete lack of the urge to possess. Love is an art and a sacrament. It serves the greatest good.

Love can only enter a house where a person lives happily alone. At the same time, an empty room should always be kept in that house, metaphorically speaking, for when the lover comes to call. So keep a chamber in your heart ready, and aired, with fresh flowers, enticing smells, and bowls of juicy fruits. A house with a room ready will guide your true love in when he enters within range. Meanwhile, the rest of the house should be full of activity – people, talk, music, cooking, all the creative pursuits of a person who is totally involved in the minutiae of their own life. Even cleaning should be done with attention. (OK, I've gone too far.) This is a person whose soulmate is on the way. Loving other people, animals, plants, even the weather, creates the kind of aura around you that attracts mates. It surrounds you in a kind of sweet smell – flowers do this without thinking. People loving you, then, is a by-product of you loving them, and everything else in the universe. You can only experience their love through your love – if you don't love a person you cannot feel their love for you. Besides, you can never really know how much anyone else loves you – nor truly believe what they say. People often talk of love just to ensure they can do what they want with you. They attract you with showy things first, hoping to collect later, like agents for Littlewoods' catalogue. The person who truly loves you does things that you will probably never even know they did. (Like sticking up for you when others are slagging you off, or cleaning up the cat sick before you get home).

People who make showy sacrifices don't truly love. They do it for the self-satisfaction of being a martyr. (Mothers can sacrifice way too much for their children – so keep this in check.) I may be wrong, and you may actually be a real live saint – the Vatican has you on their list for beatification. I doubt it though, because you're reading this book, and this is definitely a book for women who love to sin. This is a book for women who yearn.

But let's not kid ourselves that it is easy, or even possible, to love others all the time. What we do, generally, we do for ourselves, but that's fine, because our real selves are linked up on some higher plane with everyone else's, into one big groovy self. All we can do is try not to do stuff at the expense of others. Let's not imagine we can just waft around, dispensing love like hippies in filmy frocks from *Ghost*. Let's not fool ourselves that it's even possible habitually to take others into account. If we did, we could barely survive the average day. Your lunch is at someone else's expense (a cow, a pig, a chicken or several prawns). OK, so you're a smartarse vegetarian, but don't kid yourself that lettuce grew just to be in your sandwich. Your attractive shoes are at the expense of someone's hide, your stylish clothes were made in sweat shops, a dollar a day was paid to the maker of your trainers, your beautifully beaded accessories helped ruin an Indian child's eyes. Your make-up was tested on the pupils of hamsters. God only knows what is happening to entire families of furry little beasts just so you can have the drugs in your bathroom cabinet. STOP, STOP, ALREADY, you cry. But I'm not banging on to depress you, and I am guilty as charged of all. All I'm saying is, let's try not to be hypocrites. It is impossible to be good. When God made Adam and Eve, He also created within them the capacity to be bad (otherwise we'd all still be grooving about in the garden, with a soundtrack by Crosby, Stills and Nash). It is another of God's ironic little jokes. For you to live, other things must die. All you can try to do is limit the damage.

Love is a creative act, admitting you and your beloved into The Big Picture, The Master Plan. Put simply, it's always trying to do what is best spiritually for you and the other. A huge proportion of people play at love in order to get power, to which end they use the emotions of others, manipulating and employing strategies. This is soulless, and leads to mutual suffering. (Rose lace La Perla is a legitimate strategy – playing hard to get, or holding out false hope to one who yearns is not.) Players may succeed in getting people obsessed with them for a while, because we all put value on what is difficult to attain. Seduction is a strategy with simple rules – keep your partner permanently unnerved, and obsession results. But all that energy put into power games just depletes the seducer's own capacity to experience love, and they fear that once they give in and are got, they won't be wanted after all. This locks out love. Men often pretend love to get sex, and women pretend sex to get love. Each ends up feeling cheated and empty, having gained nothing at all.

Some people like to suggest that there now exists a new millennial kind of love, a more sophisticated, cynical, self-serving kind of deal. (No-one, not even the most jaded, can bear to say that love has died, proving how much we all still secretly yearn.) Men and women are more alike now, they say, and we can both do everything the other can do. The mystery of attraction has been solved. Many men actually prefer prostitutes to the effort of relationships, women have lost all respect for the male. We even consider taking up lesbianism (until we see how sapphic relationships can be just as difficult). Women now have birth control and corporate perks, men have skincare ranges and prosthetic pecs. We *all* have intimacy problems, and marriage is for mugs. To those who say we are becoming genderless, I have the following to say: you only have to watch how a man or a woman approaches the same problem – like how to shut the freezer door when it's long overdue for defrosting – to know what arrant nonsense this is. (Repeated slamming by the former, careful application of hot water by the saner.) We are intrinsically different, and love will always involve seeing the value in that. Modern romantic cynicism is a kind of fascism, the politics of the Narcissist Party. Love has not died, but merely gone underground, like the French Resistance, waiting for a kinder world.

Love means mutual giving, and always doing your best. But doing the best for someone else definitely does *not* mean giving them money, nursing them through their addictions, providing home and hearth and emotional support, just so they don't have to provide such stuff for themselves. Does your inner male need these things? No! The minute you find yourself even remotely mothering a man, you are doing him and yourself harm. (Unless he fathers you, when needed, to an equal extent.) Doing the best for someone else simply means doing what's best for their spiritual development. That may actually mean chucking them out. If helping their growth also helps yours, then soulmating is in progress.

That first great know-all, the Oracle at Delphi, said 'know thyself'. This is not so easily done as said. Knowing yourself means getting to grips with a whole roomful of rowdy and contradictory characters, all talking at once, vying for dominance and trying to drown each other out. But you really do have to have a go, even if it takes a lifetime to achieve. Those who don't know themselves can't possibly know what they want and need in someone else. The more you know yourself, the more you can help other people find out about themselves, and this is a very attractive quality indeed in a person. No relationship is so blessed as that between two people who help each other become bigger and deeper.

It's not a bad argument that fucked-up people are really the only ones who have their priorities straight. They've been to the edges of the known universe, poked about in the dark corners behind the stars, where all the creepy, scuttling things live, and have come back to tell the tale. Like Captain Kirk. You have to go there to know – to find out that life is inherently both good and evil and to discover that every life has a dark, shadowy underbelly. We are all capable of dark thoughts. We are all capable of vile deeds. This knowledge fucks you up a little, but that's the whole point of the human computer game. You start out at level one, with omnipotent baby power, but as you go on to each new level, fresh monsters attack you, and you have to survive it all and just carry on. It doesn't matter how much you get lost on the way, because all your gains will be taken from you anyway, eventually. Winning means simply finishing the game. Having someone go through all this shit with you is a great comfort, but won't in any way save you. You do it because forward is the only way to go.

These days we seem to have lost faith in simple thinking. In fact, you can only employ this to satisfying effect on your deathbed. Beatle George's last words were 'love one another', and we all got misty-eyed when we read this in the press. You couldn't go around saying *that* every day, people would take you for a fruit. But as your final words, they are pretty cool. (Start composing and practising your final words now – you never know when you might need them.) Nowadays we like to tease out the ramifications of every conceivable aspect of living, unpack the suitcase and examine every tiny item. We've all got Critical Studies degrees in Everyday Living. A simple person is an idiot. Magazines are packed with stuff you never knew you wanted, and opinions you didn't know you needed to hear, but now you think you do. At the risk of sounding like a dope, I'm with the Beatles. All you need is love – to love and be loved. All the rest is just glamour.

We think of glamour as a good thing, but look in a

dictionary and you'll see it is defined as a quality that bewitches, enchants and is illusory – i.e. not true beauty. Now, those of us who are not so natural that we can trust in our own innate beauty are going to go for all the glamour we can get at Boots, but we now live in a society that is so over-glamorised, from cars to kitchen units, that the functionality of things is barely relevant. Remember Keats – 'Truth is beauty, beauty, truth', and that is basically it.

Relying too much on your glamour to get you love is not wise. In our narcissistic age, we follow the erroneous idea that making ourselves more and more attractive physically will attract more and more love to us. In reality, it just attracts more sex. (People who get laid a lot do not seem any happier than those who don't.) While we're all so busy staring at our own reflections in each other's eyes, we've got no attention left to focus on the other person. Physical glamour is fantastically overrated – observe the rich and famous and see if they have more love. The most loved people I know are not adored for their physical appearance – but rather for the beauty that appears *through* them. Show your marvellous, truthful soul, and another beautiful soul will be attracted to yours. And if love, truth and beauty are all the same thing, it follows that you only have to exercise one and the other two will follow behind, like the wheels on a tricycle. And it can be done at any age, at any time of day, and in any place where there are other people.

A trip to the Tate Modern furnishes a good example of how much people have to complicate beauty. Artists in the past used only to see beautiful objects and to try to represent them as they saw them, truthfully, and with love. Now, however, next to the Monets and Manets, Matisses and Bonnards are piles of twisted metal, black furry squares, things with oval wheels and blow-up porno dolls. I'm not saying that these artefacts are not interesting, but many of them do seem to be the products of very tortured minds.

These are people who have lost sight of the important, simple things. They've lost the plot.

Ninety per cent of what the media portrays as real is just not true, it's all part of a confused, paranoid dream – the *mitote*, as Mexican shamans say, an unconscious conspiracy, a cultural nightmare, the matrix gone mad. And 85 per cent of this is written about love. Love and the unhappy single career woman is a hot topic in the media right now. The press cannot be trusted on this subject, because they are mostly members of this clan, writing about themselves. Spite and envy reign. The dictates of advertising rule. Features that clash with ads are just not published. You cannot tell the truth about beauty, love or sex. The entire delusory, extremely lucrative glamour industry feeds on reader insecurity, and the most successful magazines are the ones that stoke up the narcissistic paranoia to such a frenzy that you feel you must buy more and more – and it must be the latest styles. Last year's fashions in your home and you have no hope. Frilly tops and denim? *Froideur* confronts you. Shaker kitchen units? *Schadenfreude* will come to call. NEW stuff, fashionable stuff, glamorous stuff – this is offered as a substitute for love. The most discontented people in the world are fashion and style journalists. Just look into their eyes – their lizard handbags have more warmth.

So what hope is there for the single older woman? Once upon a time a woman had a husband, children, an extended family, and maybe an outside friend or two if she was lucky. Sounds cosy, huh? But she was often totally pissed off with all of these people, and they with her. In olden days women died in childbirth, went mad, took to their beds, caught pneumonia or consumption – anything rather than live out a lifespan with that set of demands. In the fifties, she kept going with booze and valium, and ever more frantic attempts to clean the kitchen floor. Only crazy, clever or ugly women chose a different route.

Today, lots of women don't have husbands, or they might have had two or three, and many don't have children either. They may have divorced their parents and siblings because they don't like them, and moved hundreds, sometimes thousands of miles to get away from them. The old folk, if they look like living on too long, are put in homes. But what a modern single woman does have now is loads of friends, and several people in her life that she does actually love. She also has her own home that she paid for herself, and, hopefully, work she enjoys. Is this lone woman happier, unhappier or just the same as before?

We are informed that this woman is more lonely and miserable than ever. Well, take a look at your own mother. Need I say more? Despite the lack of partners, never mind soulmates, no, we are not unhappier. We just want it all, and we believe it is achievable, if only we can work out how to get it. 'Having it all' no longer means material assets, but emotional ones. We are trying to create real, honest relationships, 'Real Love' from scratch. It's the mission of modern women everywhere. Even if we never do find our soulmates, it's up to us to show men how to employ the power of love, not the love of power. Moses went up and got the tablets of stone. There is no bloke up on a mountain to help us this time, and the only incendiary Bush that can speak transmits tripe from America. No, we've got to carve it all out for ourselves. We're in crisis because we are suffering from a lack of love. It is the job of women to re-introduce this atmosphere into the male-female equation. The Goddess, She-Who-Must-Be-Obeyed, must return. Perhaps in ancient pagan cultures, men and women did know how to love each other. Early Christian Gnostics held naked outdoor love-ins, apparently, that made our rock festivals look like an evening at the Wigmore Hall. Women were regarded as equal to men, in every way, and Jesus had his female equivalent, Sophia. Unfortunately, they didn't leave any self-help books behind. (Although The Dead Sea Scrolls are said to be full of mind-bogglingly sexy and exuberant stuff.) By the time we got to The Bible, bearded men had already taken over, Sophia had gone underground and madonna or magdalena (i.e. saint or whore) were the only versions of womankind left.

We all want soulmates, and we all want love. So far so good, but then it can quickly turn sour. Because we want love to come with other stuff, such as gifts, good looks, flat stomachs, or, at the very least, hair. We are so nasty about each other. The way we describe people we are rejecting is murderous. TV makeover shows home in on our sadistic nature, throwing poor innocents into the arena to be slaughtered, all of whom started out looking like themselves, and end up looking like GMTV weather girls. We break down everything about a person into separate components to explain why they are all wrong and a failure by the standards of cultural hegemony. Then we are surrounded by tawdry images of sex, reducing it to a trashy entertainment, totally separate from love. Well, try sex with someone you love, and someone you don't. Be honest now. The former will remain something that you will never ever regret. It had spontaneity, it was harmonious, you never felt more alive. Now think of all the sex you've had with people you didn't love. No matter how many techniques and gadgets were involved, it was a grim exercise, *n'est-ce pas*? Something you'd rather forget – if you can bear a mental reconstruction at all. There is an acrid taste, the colours are murky, the atmosphere impure. You probably only did it because there was no love available to you at the time. Perhaps you wanted to check that you could still pull. Or you didn't want to be alone on a bank holiday. It can take an awful lot of bad sex for some people finally to accept the inevitable. A lot of poor children are born of this bad sex, and the consequences for them and the planet are dire.

Yes, BUT . . . I hear you say, what about everything you said in an earlier chapter about sex with friends and not falling in love with them?

OK. Let's define 'In Love' and 'Love'. People remonstrate hard to defend their right to be 'In Love'. But 'In Love' is a dodgy state. It happens when one projects and invests so much in another person that one's own sense of identity depends on the other's perfection. In the company of the beloved, you feel like the person you would like to be. You have become as one, and because the beloved is peerless and pure, *ipso facto* so are you. It's a darned clever narcissistic trick. Planet Janet is now Janet and John. Everything that lives and grows on this planet has janetness and johnity, regardless of whether this is a nice place to be. 'In Love' is an ego state. How many times have you heard celebrities braying how much in love they are, only to see them divorce in the most unbelievable acrimony a few months down the line? There may be mutuality when 'In Love', but this is because you are both feeding the same ego monster. This is not the same as simply loving someone. You love your friends – i.e. you try to do what is best for their spiritual development at all times (see above). But you are separate entities, planets revolving merrily together round the sun, but with separate trajectories, that sometimes cross and sometimes don't. You have an affinity. You have not exploded into one. You do not inhabit a separate superior universe of two, but enjoy the experience of this one flawed universe together. So if you are going to enjoy sex with friends while waiting for your soulmate, don't see this as second best, and try to make sure you do it with friends you love. Just don't try to turn them into soulmates, or get disappointed that they are not He, or denigrate them for not being as rich or as beautiful as you think you deserve. The two greatest sex-and-beauty icons of the twentieth century, Marilyn and Elvis, both died alone, and never found their soulmates, much as they tried. This was because all that phoney, distracting adulation took up so much time, they couldn't get round to hunting for themselves. Marilyn was so busy being the ultimate female that her inner male, with nothing to do, went into a coma. Soulmates have no connection with beauty or wealth. They have everything to do with acknowledging the needs of one's own soul. You can't turn someone into one by sheer dint of effort. If you're having sex with a friend, and it's going OK, and fundamentally there is love and respect, then carry on, no questions asked.

Now you have an inkling of what a soulmate is – how to meet yours? Enough tomes to fill the ancient library at Alexandria have been written about this. Burn them all again. There is only one simple rule. GET OUT MORE. Young singletons will go anywhere rather than stay in on a Saturday night, then they slumber on till 4 p.m., totally shagged out from the night before, happily bypassing the sombre rigours of the standard Sunday morning.

Looking out of my window as I write, *men are everywhere.* There are several outside my window right now, doing something incredibly noisy with a cement mixer. Two more strapping topless types are moving bricks from one pile to another about six feet apart. (Who knows why?) There's one in a white cowboy hat strolling past, an intriguingly sinister black rider is parking his motorbike. One actually came inside my house about an hour ago to mend my dryer. Another stopped by last night while hiding from the police. (A misunderstanding, he assured me.) Earlier today, a neighbour hailed me in the street with 'Mornin' gorgeous' as I staggered to the corner to buy milk. OK, he lied, but oh, how sweet and kind men can be. Last week another helped me with a heavy suitcase. So just get out more, and *talk to them.* Women who have lots of men in their lives are women who talk to strangers. When we say people don't talk to strangers any more, what we actually mean is that men don't talk to women (unless they're drunk, then they *sing*). Men are much too terrified to talk to us, because they don't want to be accused of being perverts or stalkers. (Although one did ask my advice yesterday, uninvited, while choosing some shoes in Barratts, and ended up telling me some passably funny jokes. In return, I steered him away from some highly unsuitable grey trainers.) As long as you don't allow stray men (who might be weird) into your home, what have you got to lose? Men are often so starved of female chat, that when introduced to you formally they usually deliver their entire life history, with full intimate revelations, immediately. So to every man you meet, just be friendly, be kind. A young friend doing a survey on personal ads for her psychology degree found that what men valued most in women, surprisingly, wasn't 34DD, but kindness. OK, you might get some dodgy date offers, but you can always decline them kindly. (Three men in my street want to date me simply because I talk to them, and I only do that because I believe in being neighbourly, which seems to be a very eccentric concept these days.)

By now, you may be thinking that I am posing as some kind of idiot savant. Talk to men and try to love them. At any age, that's all it takes. Oh, *come on*! The naiveté! But I'm not saying that there won't still be tears. Love and tears go together like tequila and salt. But tears shed in love pain are more exquisite than tears shed in boredom, or the tears I often shed in Sainsbury's at the sheer, overpowering awfulness of it all. Love pain tears are the tears of the soul. Avoiding love pain is the anaesthetised way we live now, just as we avoid physical discomfort, facing up to stuff, and taking the difficult path. We are spineless and spoon-fed, and we don't have the grit. So strap on your quiver, fill it with arrows, and get out there a' hunting. Keep a model of the hunter goddess, Diana, on your mantelpiece, to remind you of your quest. (Or take up archery – the instructor needs to stand *very* close behind you while adjusting your aim.)

To Sum Up

To find out what your *animus* is like, ask yourself, what do you like and not like in men? Then ask yourself, what perhaps, do men like and not like in you?

Here is a summary, courtesy of my undergraduate friend's research, of some of the negative stuff women see in men. *Lazy, selfish, egotistical, crude, aggressive, unreliable, moody, mean, jealous, using, non-committal, controlling, lying, OAFS.*

Here is a summary of the negative stuff men see in some of us. *Bossy, whining, gold-digging, judgemental, humourless, unromantic, clinging, controlling, possessive, bitchy, manipulative, HARRIDANS.*

Here is the positive stuff men see in women. *Kind, gentle, affectionate, supportive, soft, strong, beautiful, ANGELS.*

This is the positive stuff we look for in men. *Funny, generous, good-natured, courageous, strong, loyal, HEROES.*

It follows then, that your soulmate will be the one who liberates your inner *angel*, and puts your inner *harridan* behind bars. You will summon forth his *hero*, and bury his inner *oaf*.

If a man supports your soul, helps you discover yourself, is interested in what you have to say, laughs at your jokes, likes the way you look without make-up and strong underwear, and can join in most activities with you without getting irritable, soulmating is underway. But first and foremost, before you are a woman and he is a man, you've both got to become fully human, and very rarely is this possible until *at least* mid-life. So don't for one minute think it's all over for you – in fact it's only just begun. Unity Beckons.

If you think all this spiritual soulmate stuff is just so much hairy-legged, earth motherly navel-gazing, let me recommend to you an alternative route, the Rita Roberts book *Soul Mates*. Described as Princess Diana's favourite medium (and, arguably, by the nature of her calling, she still is), Rita says that you really don't have to do anything at all to find your soulmate, because dead relatives on the other side are sorting it all out for you, looking on, sending messages through mediums, pulling strings and wangling things so that you and your soulmate will eventually meet. Should this, to your mind, seem much more likely, and generally more in keeping with your busy lifestyle (plus you don't even have to *pay* a match-making agency of the dead), I wish you all the luck in the world, and plenty of patience while you wait.

'If the Master doesn't arrive in five more minutes, this mistress is going to turn into a mattress . . .'

5
The Mistress

Wendy Salisbury

Reclining on a velvet damask chaise longue, the marabou fur trim around her satin negligée gently caressing the soft skin of her fragrant décolletage, the mistress languidly sips champagne as she waits for her lover to call . . . She smiles as she remembers his last visit, his gift of a diamond bracelet, his promise that soon they would be together, his ecstasy as their passion reached its peak. As she glances at the clock, she realises that the hour is now late and his appearance this evening is unlikely. She rises up with a sigh, replaces the half-drunk bottle in the fridge and prepares herself, once more, for her solitary bed.

What is a mistress? The female version of a master? *He* is defined as someone who has authority, who is in control, the head of a household or a college, a ship's captain, a skilled craftsman, the holder of a university degree higher than bachelor, the owner of an animal or slave, the director of hounds at a hunt, the presiding officer in a masonic lodge or institution. *She* is defined as a 'woman having illicit sex with a (married) man'. I could rest my case here, but I won't. A master is also an 'original from which copies can be made', which conjures up a pile of pale, feint, dilute descendants of Adam, in other words – men. The inference in the definitions is clear: one commands, the other submits. But which, in reality, is which?

The 'master' is usually a married man committed to one woman for the benefit of society, propriety and propagation. He soon notices that having made the right little go-er who was his fiancée into his wife, her desire for him fades as fast as the flowers in the wedding bouquet. The amoral fun and frolics they once snatched in the back seats of cars and cinemas have been relegated to a fortnightly nightie-round-the-waist duty performance filed by her under the category of 'bedroom unpleasantness'. He gazes beyond the harbour walls and sees the Sirens swaying on the rocks. He is so seduced by their beauty and song that he slips into the water and swims towards them ignoring the unseen dangers lurking in the depths . . .

The mistress in history was a significant and provocative creature, an astute and cunning mademoiselle or madame who knew the value of her charms and milked them to the max. The pussy power that she engendered has provided vicarious thrills, *frissons* and fascination to generations of gossips ever since Cleopatra let Julius Caesar slip out through one curtain and ushered in Mark Antony through the other. Although they may differ from each other in looks and aspirations (some rough-and-ready wenches content with a roll in the hay and a slap on the arse, other great beauties demanding nothing less than a nation as compensation), any mistress worth her salt should know that her lover, God bless him, no matter his position in the hierarchy of world power, is a weak and impressionable soul much taken with a well-turned ankle or a blinding blow job (go, Monica . . .). In many cultures, the mistress is an accepted and even expected member of the community, an integral part of the body politic. A man would agree to an arranged marriage for the sole purpose of appeasing the parents and producing children to carry on the family line. It would be considered almost improper for him to enjoy sex with his wife and he was expected to find pleasure elsewhere. In Japan, they have their Geisha, deep-rooted in the tradition of Far Eastern inscrutability. Trained from the age of puberty in the art of 'gent-ertainment', she acts as an antithesis to the wife – sexy and witty, as opposed to quotidian and serious. An undemanding and compliant hospitality hostess, she is there to pleasure her master, flatter his ego, fawn at his feet, and dispense tea and sympathy from behind a painted smile. In the Middle East, as if four wives were not enough, they have their Harem filled to the brim with available totty – exotic, erotic, and ready-to-roll at the clash of a cymbal. And they don't even have to be taken out for dinner. India gave us the *Kama Sutra*, that most earthy and spicy sex manual, which must have taken hours of practice and a coterie of double-jointed volunteers to perfect. For sure, Mrs Vatsyayana was not the only participant. 'Get your left leg off my right shoulder, you Tantric tosser, I'm cooking your curry', was probably her answer to some of the old man's more risqué suggestions. In Italy, if a man is monogamous, he is considered a wuss, and when you look at some of the voluptuous and beautiful women his country has produced (Sophia Loren, Gina Lollobrigida, Monica Vitti) is it any wonder Marcello Mastroianni wanted to have his *pannetonne* and eat it? In France, they have their *cinq à sept*, the commonly accepted time of day when extra-marital afternoon delight is mutually indulged. In fact, the French win hands (and knees) down in the adultery department having produced the *grande dame* of all royal mistresses – Madame de Pompadour: overdressed, overindulged and overjoyed to provide sexual overkill to Louis XV. Today's mistress might aspire to a *pied-à-terre* with a good postcode – that clever *cocotte* got Versailles. If Louis wanted theatre, she'd ask Molière to write him a play in which she would star. If Louis wanted furniture, she'd assemble the finest craftsmen and cabinet-makers of the day – no pushing a trolley round

IKEA for this little lady. She changed the face and taste of the eighteenth century with her gilded rococo, hand-crafted porcelain, and jewel-encrusted *objets de vertu*, all commissioned to mirror the beauty and bounty of the Alphababe herself. Lowly locals of the time would thrust their sisters, daughters and even wives into the path of a passing nobleman or prince in the hopes that a similar good fortune would rub off on them and that young Fanny would be lapped up, thereby assuring wealth and comfort for her relatives for ever. And if she managed to get right-royally knocked up, the little bastard usually got a Dukedom as a christening present.

It all sounds like nice work if you can get it: the mistress has the best of him, the wife gets the rest of him. So is this the way forward for us sexy, single sirens? Inside every one of us, is there an inherent seductress writhing to get out – a brazen hussy descended not from Eve as Goodness Personified (before the incident at the greengrocer's), but from Salome, that sex-mad slut with an accessories habit who demanded nothing less than some poor John's balls (OK, head) on a plate? No matter their class or creed, these foxy ladies' common bond is a burning ambition to rise from bit-part player to centre-stage star in their upwardly-mobile quest to attract the man of their dreams and schemes. The palaces, jewels, dominions and even thrones that our sisters in sin strove for were all earned in that most revered and reviled position as *grandes horizontales* to some of the world's most famous and influential men. Regal scandals are nothing new. There is a long history of royal mistresses who recognised that they have something HM wants. Even the thirteen-year-old Nell Gwynn knew that. Selling oranges and favours to the nobility in seventeenth-century Covent Garden was just a springboard to higher things. From hooker to actress, she screwed her way through the ranks to become the favourite mistress of King

Charles II, although she nearly blew it on their first date by asking him for 'cash up front'. She bore him two sons, earned his enduring affection and found her own fame immortalised in story and song (not to mention a block of flats in Chelsea). She may have been a whore, but at least she was 'The King's Whore'.

The other woman will always cry herself to sleep
The other woman will never have his love to keep
And as the years go by, the other woman
Will spend her life alone.

(Nina Simone)

The role of the mistress is a tragi-comic one: she should have one of those smiley/frowny theatre masks above the door to remind her of her job description. It's a now-you-see-him-now-you-don't kind of world contrasted by champagne and whipped cream licked from her cleavage one minute, to dry toast and tears digested alone the next. The mistress is, and always has been, employed to provide unbridled sexual pleasure, excitement, entertainment, and admiration for a man who is prepared to be generous in his appreciation thereof. She'd probably settle for less stuff and more love, but as Tina Turner so rightly said 'What's love got to do with it?' Love is what he feels for his wife, his children, his business, his Bentley, his bar stool, his golf clubs. Furs, jewellery, apartments, travel, cars and designer clothes are what keep the mistress warm at night, the stock-in-trade of the well-kept woman. She may have been a prostitute, a model, a showgirl, a shop assistant, an actress or a secretary but she sure learns fast how to improve her living conditions. The Hollywood movie-type had her own maid, cook and chauffeur but that is a bit aspirational these days (you really can't get the staff). Yet deep at the bottom of her ever-hopeful heart, on those cold and lonely nights when he has left her to return to Her, the mistress yearns for that band of gold, to fulfil her desire to win that man and make him her own. She shouldn't dwell on it. As Sir Jimmy Goldsmith observed (and he had a few), 'The man who marries his mistress creates a job vacancy'.

There are a number of mechanical devices that increase sexual arousal in women, chief among these being the Mercedes-Benz 380SL convertible.

(PJ O'Rourke)

A clever mistress, like a winter-wise squirrel, should gather acorns while she may. Whenever he asks, 'Do you need anything?' (and he will, because he feels guilty) hold your hand out with a coy little smile and say, 'Oh, darling, you shouldn't, but I did see the most divine . . .' This will justify and empower him. If he gives you £500 for new clothes, spend £150 and bank the rest. It isn't difficult to look gorgeous on a budget, all the secretaries in his office do it and they have far less brains than you. Although not easy, you must accept that you will be spending some birthdays alone, along with Christmas, New Year, weekends and bank holidays. This is not something to baulk at, you knew from the outset that it goes with the territory. Make sure you have a network of good friends to fill these lonely times, or you will become angry and resentful, and that is not the face he wants to see when he knocks at your door. That's the face he left behind at home, and one of the reasons he is coming to see you. Depending on your age, the biological clock may be ticking and you will have to decide whether or not to make this an issue. The mistress who gets pregnant 'by accident' is often asked to get rid of it. Either way, she will often be dumped or paid off. Having a baby will completely upset the balance of the relationship and he's probably been there, done that, wiped the puke off the T-shirt, and is getting ready to become a grandfather. Do it for yourself, if you must, but be prepared to bring the love-child up as an embittered mouthy one-parent family.

My wife is a sex object – every time I ask for sex, she objects.
(Rodney D.)

Rejoice that you do not have him around 24/7, for that is the stuff of complacency. Half the appeal of the relationship is its infrequency, the struggle to spend time together, the disappointment of a cancellation sweetened by the anticipation of the next assignation. Every occasion is a honeymoon, every snatched afternoon or evening a magical interlude when everything is centred around you, you and only you and the sex is the best that money can buy. To many women, being fêted, admired and adored in short bursts is infinitely more appealing than the monotony of monogamy with all its tedious repetition and lacklustre predictability. A wife bears many stresses and strains on her body and brain: childbearing, child rearing, balancing the budget, maintaining a career, sucking up to his family, shopping, cooking, cleaning – no wonder she's too shagged out to shag him. And so he turns to you to bewitch and beguile him away from dull domesticity into a magical world where everything is pleasure and pleasure is everything.

Ironically, although by its very nature the post of devoted mistress is an unfaithful pastime, fidelity and trust are a requirement. He will expect total commitment, round the clock availability, sycophantic flattery and supine selflessness. She will be expected to lie to whoever necessary to make time to be together, the stories becoming ever more inventive the more they get away with it and as the affair gathers pace. If they are both office-based, she may find herself telling *his* wife that he's 'working late' while he's actually under the desk with his face up her skirt. One boss liked to go to meetings with his secretary's knickers in his pocket, until he pulled them out one day to mop his brow, much to the amusement of the other directors round the table. On these occasions, men get the thumbs-up and a round of applause from their peers, while the woman is denigrated, vilified and branded a tart – the usual male/female imbalance of the sexual scales. The risks and sacrifices she has to make are not taken into consideration. She may have to point out some home truths to him, in the gentlest possible way. Apart from her body, she is giving him her time, her status and her youth, high prizes not to be given away without due recompense. For an ongoing affair, the minimum price, in the absence of a wedding ring and the right to half his estate, should be a good address in her own name at the very least.

Mistresses fall into two categories – victims and vixens. For a single or even attached woman, the flattering attentions of a married man are a real head-spinner, especially if he is Rich and Powerful. These two attributes are key. They will drive the relationship and act as an aphrodisiac – even if he looks like a frog and humps like a camel. The vixen will not give a passing thought to the fact that he's married – *she* hasn't taken the vows so they're not her problem. She will seduce him away from his hearth and home with impunity – a ruthless temptress and conniving opportunist. The power she has to obsess and possess him is her driving force, a duplicitous, complicitous creature bent on aggrandisement, unfazed by her tag of 'home-wrecker'. The mistress as victim is a gullible girl who gets sucked into a world of sophistication far removed from her original roots. Her freshness and innocence are her main attractions and he will want to play Svengali to her Trilby, show off his world and revisit it through her eyes. For him it's a double whammy. He gets to play God and the Devil in one, reaping her gratitude, devotion, and reverence mixed with insecurity – what greater power kick for any man? She will fall deeply in love with him, succumb to his every whim and believe all the promises he ever makes her. She truly accepts that if she loves him enough, the power of that love will conquer all and he will eliminate the past and make her his present, and future. And he plays along – after all, why shouldn't he? He can afford to buy the best of both worlds. He assures her that he will leave his wife 'when his son is sixteen, when his daughter gets married, when that big deal comes off, when his golf handicap reaches single figures, when his elderly mother dies' . . . when pigs fly, when men don't lie, when his nose grows so long it snaps right off at the root. *He will never leave his wife.* He may be crazy but he is not stupid. To give up the shared family history and secure background to start all over again in later life with some nymphet who happened to take his fancy is just far too much hassle and way too expensive, and what was once a charming insinuation is now beginning to sound like a monotonous nag. No matter what he says in the sack, he will always be aware of the cost of divorce in both material and emotional terms. Men are cowards, they abhor confrontation and would rather change their mistress for a less-demanding model than lose everything they have ever worked for, together with their standing in the community. Be she vixen or victim, the mistress may well miss the marriage boat, grow old and dry and change her name to Havisham before she ever sees her wedding day. Living on hopes and promises is living a dream. Even the beautiful world-famous opera diva, Maria Callas, long-time lover of the world's richest man, could not get Aristotle Onassis to marry her. She craved a husband and a normal family life, but all she got were parties, nightclubs and cruises, dying aged fifty-three, unhappy and alone, after he dissed her in the most insulting way by marrying the world's most eligible widow, Jackie Kennedy. And Marilyn Monroe, surely the ultimate sex goddess and fantasy female for all generations got passed around the Kennedy clan like an old baseball glove and was never given the respect she deserved, dying in mysterious circumstances and not (it has been alleged) by her own hand.

The clever mistress should always use her brains gift-wrapped in her beauty as she climbs the slippery ladder to sex-cess. In the post-coital afterglow of two relaxed heads sharing the same pillow, secrets and revelations may slip from loose tongues, awarding the careful listener the opportunity for advancement. That is what made Christine Keeler such a threat in the Swinging Sixties. While pleasuring Her Majesty's Secretary of State for War, John Profumo, she was also dancing the horizontal *kazutzki* with Soviet naval attaché, Captain Eugene Ivanov, and although not very bright, the politicos thought she ticked like a time bomb. All she wanted was what all women want – the love, affection and support of a kind and caring man. What she got was a prison sentence for perjury and the scorn of a nation. Some other historically-famous mistresses were not that well-endowed in the physics department but beavered away on the chemistry front proving that prowess in the bedroom could mean power in the boardroom. Wallis Simpson could hardly have been called a looker but she managed to lure King Edward VIII from his throne by performing a series of juicy stunts she'd allegedly picked up in a Shanghai brothel. (This is hearsay, but it sounds dead racy, don't you think?) Becoming his bosom buddy, a sympathetic listener, a patient advisor, a shoulder to cry on and an unswerving support through the sort of crisis not many of us encounter in our everyday lives, there was clearly no contest. For a shy and sexually insecure man, the question 'To be or not to be . . . King?' was easy to answer. 'I'll take the Shanghai Shagger, please, Stanley,' and so changed the course of British history. The Princes of Wales through the ages have clearly been a randy and promiscuous lot. Edward VII counted at least six famous fillies among his collection of fancy women. The queen of melodrama, 'The Divine' Sarah Bernhardt, had an affair with him that continued on and off for twenty years. She received a special invitation to his coronation in Westminster Abbey and found herself sitting next to another of his mistresses, one Alice Keppel, Camilla Parker Bowles's great-granny. He also dallied with artist's model Lillie Langtry, for whom he built a most sumptuous villa. Just to keep it in the family, Lillie later became the mistress of Lord Louis Mountbatten (Prince Philip's grandfather), by whom she had a daughter. *Droit de seigneur* rules, OK? The chattering classes were much entertained and envious of the power (behind the throne) that these clandestine but celebrated sweeties possessed. In some cases, the official wives condoned the relationship, glad to relinquish the sexual demands of their husbands to 'the other woman'. The afore-mentioned Alice Keppel was often summoned by Queen Alexandra to calm the king and improve his mood so he could attend better to his Affairs of State, 'affairs' being the operative word. Mrs Keppel was personally escorted by the queen to visit 'Kingy' on his deathbed. In more modern times, Françoise Gilot, a girl who enjoyed the company of painters, became Picasso's greatest inspiration, although I do wonder why she didn't get him to pay for corrective surgery to re-align her weirdly asymmetrical face. He was as perverse as his art, telling her off for submitting to his advances on the grounds that he could not seduce her if she wasn't going to resist him. (Huh?)

*You may have your legs in the air but you must keep your
feet on the ground.*

(WS)

The secret of a rich and fruitful life as a mistress is to (appear
to) relinquish your independence and totally acquiesce to
His Master's Voice. As a confidante you must listen to his
blather with unerring fascination, be it about high finance,
trouble a' t' mill, or the sodding school fees. You may not
give a flying fuck about the price of pork bellies, but that
Chanel suit with matching shoes and bag could depend on
it, so pay attention and praise him for being so knowledge-
able. The sweetest music a mistress will ever hear is when
her lover disses his wife and complains about his home life.
These revelations will warm you like a cashmere blanket on
a cold night: the children's bad behaviour, how untidy his
house is, what a lousy meal she cooked last night and how
she never listens to a word he says. Talk to me, baby, tell me
all about it . . . and of course, how he *never has sex at home any
more.* Married men NEVER have sex at home any more, or
so they say. Don't you believe it. They have sex wherever
they can get it. The confidences he shares with you will go
straight into your Hope Chest and in time, he may trust you
enough to include you in outside activities, which you will
interpret as building blocks to a stronger relationship. This
does not mean that by going public he is going to leave her
and marry you. It simply means that he is getting cocky. The
more he gets away with, the more risks he takes, and, of
course, there is an unspoken agreement between the males
of the species not to rat on their fellow infidels. He will want
to show you off as a mark of his masculinity, an extra-
curricular feather in his sexual cap. Never let him down, for
although his peers will presume what you are in the
bedroom, you are not expected to prove it in the ballroom.
Getting pissed and flirting with his work colleagues is not a

good idea. You are his possession and if you wish to retain the status quo, you have to behave yourself. Make him proud of you and an expensive 'thank you' should ensue.

Sex is one of the most wholesome, beautiful and natural experiences that money can buy.

(*Steve Martin*)

Great sex and plenty of it is the catalyst between the lover and his *amoureuse* and their every meeting will reflect this fact in all its forms and fantasies. Whether you feel like it or not, every time has to be Showtime with all the make-up, costume and accessories that this role demands. Stockings, suspenders, crotchless knickers, peep-hole bras, camisoles, basques, bustiers, garters, thigh boots, stilettos and assorted battery-operated equipment must become an integral part of your wardrobe. All men have horny fantasies about sex-mad strippers and lascivious lap-dancers so, if it pleases His Majesty, that is what you must become. If, like most mistresses, you can't bear the thought of him doing it with his wife, just console yourself with this: while you are cavorting around the room dressed like a stunt double for Nicole Kidman in *Moulin Rouge*, she is attending a parents-teachers meeting. While you are being tied up with silk cords and rogered doggie-fashion, she is trussing a chicken and stuffing Paxo up its arse. While you are peeling off his pants and massaging his ego with scented oils, she is peeling potatoes and pouring Mazola into a frying-pan. While you are lying moist and sated on your satin sheets, she is shovelling shirts into the washing-machine. Still wanna be his wife?

As a sex object/slave, you will need to learn as many tricks as a street magician to keep him interested and entertained. Even if some of these antics are not your scene, you must pretend to be enjoying them Big Time. At some point, he will probably ask if you have a girlfriend you could invite along to make up a threesome. This may not be your particular penchant, but it has always been his. Your immediate reaction will be one of jealousy, hurt that you alone are not enough for him any more. He will deny this and will promise you that:

(a) he'll 'look after' you (interpret this as you will),
(b) he won't perform penetration with the other girl and
(c) he just wants to watch.

Don't believe any of it. The best way of dealing with his suggestion is to talk about it. All the time. Face to face, back to back, before, during and after sex, by phone, text and e-mail. It will drive him nuts, act as foreplay, and keep him in a constant state of suspended animation. Unless you really want to, delay the evil day. Include her when you are making love, describing what you would do to her if she were there. This may be enough for the both of you and the reality will never be as good as the fantasy anyway. If you do decide to go ahead, you will need to select either a complete stranger (see *Yellow Pages*) or a girlfriend you trust implicitly with whom you can practise some form of fake fuckery (or fuck fakery). Either way, you will need a lot of vodka.

It is not news that the male of the species has capricious tendencies, in the Latin sense of the word – he's a goat. He may be king of his own castle but his trusty thrusty sword will lead him to crusade and conquer beyond the castle walls. He will require a retinue of scullery-maids, serving wenches, cooks, courtesans and other men's wives before he is satisfied and his carnal urges are met. With this in mind, it seems obvious that sharing becomes inevitable. Those who cannot accept this (and really, why the hell should we?) and make a big production out of throwing him out, burning his Savile Row suits and pouring his vintage Pétrus into his shoes are fighting an immovable force. They may instil sympathy and a strong sense of sisterhood from the hordes of humiliated women who went before them, but ultimately they will be pitied and probably end up alone. Men consider us interchangeable, disposable, dispensable. They will lie and deny to keep all their balls in the air at the same time. Even if this fails, he still ends up the victor, with at least one woman to keep him warm on a winter's night. The wronged wives who turn a blind eye, retain their status, their dignity and their errant husbands are the clever ones (Hillary Clinton, Mary Archer, Mrs Alan Clark). They have accepted one of life's truisms: men need their kicks, obey their dicks and dip their wicks.

If you are married, the flight to infidelity is a heady one, raising you above and beyond the boundaries of your normal existence. The dangers involved, the lure of the forbidden and the risk of discovery all add a powerful piquancy to the status quo, as do the secrets and lies that, for some nefarious reason, make an affair so appealing. It will play havoc with your sensible side as you throw knickers and caution to the wind on your sex-crazed mission for self-fulfilment. Your imagination develops a sixth dimension, creating outlandish excuses like, 'The Accounts Manager ate a bad prawn at lunchtime so *I* had to take the entire Marketing Department on the London Eye and then out to dinner because we did that last year for Admin and it didn't seem fair . . .' and the story just grows in the telling. You will need a good memory and a trusty confidante to act as cover for you. For the benefit of the person you are deceiving, this friend should be going through some sort of undefined ongoing emotional trauma that requires your undivided attention three times a week and twice on Saturdays. Always make sure *they* know that *you've* said you are with *them* when, in fact, you are with *him*, so *they* don't turn up at *yours* when *you* are meant to be with *them* (I told you it was complicated). Your moods will swing violently, depending on how well or badly it's going, and this will probably be noticed by those around you. A sudden urge to rush out and buy a loaf of bread following an off-peak text message will seem odd to all but the densest of partners, although a girl I knew once slipped out of the house for a quickie one Sunday afternoon while her husband dozed in front of the TV. On her return, having hyperventilated all the way home thinking up believable excuses, she was relieved to find him still asleep in his chair . . .

He later 'woke up', found her out and threw her out.

If you fancy the role of the mistress, you will be in good company but be aware of the dangers. For all the champagne drunk together, there will be much drunk alone, as you wait endlessly in your hotel suite for him to extricate himself from some prior engagement while your Agent Provocateur lingerie goes unruffled and unripped. You will need understanding friends who are prepared to be dumped at a moment's notice when he calls to say he's free for an hour NOW. There will be an imbalance between his dominance and your servitude, although this can be redressed between the sheets where you will often have the upper hand. And remember, the married man is always looking at his watch. Make sure that you too have a watch to look at. And insist that it's Cartier. If this is your chosen route, look out for the potholes, but walk it with pride in the highest pair of killer heels you can find.

Marla's Story

(Only the names have been changed to protect the guilty.)
Marla and Emil first met at a Fashion Fair in Bologna. They were browsing at the same stand and he inadvertently backed into her. As he turned and grabbed her arm to save her from falling, Marla looked straight into a pair of Omar Sharif-type treacle-brown eyes with long silky lashes. She noted the luxuriant, dark hair just greying at the temples and inhaled the rich, heady aroma of

Havana cigars and Monsieur Givenchy. Her heart stopped for a moment, then began beating again very fast. Emil was profuse in his apologies and insisted that she join him for a drink in the bar of his hotel, 'so I can make sure you are all right.' His continental accent provided an additional allure and, despite her better judgement, Marla accepted, for she recognised a chemistry that comes along only rarely. She presumed he was married and, of course, she was right . . . As they clinked glasses later that evening, Marla felt a lustful attraction and a visceral longing that could only be dealt with in one way. Drinks turned into dinner, during which they shared the first of many bottles of Dom Perignon rosé champagne. They talked, he teased and Marla revelled in his attention and worldly savoir faire. When he suggested a night-club, she was delighted, keen to prolong the flirtatious foreplay, wondering how it would end and where it would lead. Every ballad ever written was played for them that night. As he led her to the dance floor, the romance of the moment swept her away and she felt like a kid again. A fluttering, quivering teenager replaced the confident woman who had left home only hours earlier on a business trip, and got mixed up in some other business altogether.

In the early hours of the next morning, having made virtual love on the tiny, packed dance floor, they returned to his hotel suite and made real love in that tender yet desperate way that only happens the first time, or in the case of a tragic parting, the last time. Marla's orgasm was so intense that she knew he'd possessed her and would possess her forever.

On returning to London, they continued their affair, their desire for each other growing in intensity as their obsession took hold. Marla dropped everything to be at his side wherever and whenever he was able. Her home life and work suffered and she was dismissed from her job. Emil employed her as buyer for his fashion chain, which gave them the perfect opportunity to work and travel together: Venice on the Orient Express, where they made love four times in four countries in twenty-four hours, New York by Concorde, where he made her wear a wig and cross the street when he saw some friends approaching, St Barts on a private yacht, where he romanced her on the deck, in the Caribbean, on the beach, under the stars . . . The more they got away with, the more they dared; the more they dared, the more they wanted . . . Gifts from designer shops and the fine jewellers of Bond Street and Faubourg St Honoré were bestowed upon her – icing on the cake that Marla devoured each day. But Emil's quiet homely wife had noticed the change in him, his weight loss, his newly acquired wardrobe, the increasing excuses of 'working late', the time he spent at home deep in thought, or locked in his study making cassette tapes of international love songs. She began appearing at the office, 'taking an interest' as she put it, and Marla found herself having to lie to her about why she was away so much, and always at the same time as Emil. She invented an ailing relative in France, who became so realistic Marla actually believed she existed. One day the wife spat a warning at her, which made Marla stop and think, but she was in too deep to let it go.

Emil rented a little love nest halfway between their two homes where they could meet at every opportunity. The sex became more passionate, more urgent, as necessary for them both as breathing. They had furious arguments when he wrongfully accused her of flirting with other men, and he nearly drove them both off a cliff in Switzerland one night, so incensed was he having thought she'd smiled at a man in a bar while Emil's back was turned. The more volatile his temperament, the most passionate their reconciliations. They swore undying love for each other and she cried many tears of frustration and fear whenever they parted and he went home to his wife and family. But still their ardour raged like a forest fire that could not be extinguished.

For his fortieth birthday, she arranged for him a day of sexual hedonism and indulgence – 'a day like no day has been nor will be again'. She hired two beautiful Oriental girls to entertain him. They danced and sang for him, then undressed each other and bathed together while he and Marla soaped and stroked their satiny skin. They showered him, tantalising his senses with their naked glowing youth. Marla watched, tormented with jealousy knowing how much he was enjoying this. Then she joined them in their king-size bed as they oiled each other's bodies and massaged his with their own. She allowed them to pleasure him until he had three mouths kissing him, three tongues licking him, six breasts and more to enjoy. They watched the girls make love to each other until they could hardly breathe with the excitement of it. But penetration was reserved for Marla . . . that was the one and only rule that crazy afternoon. When the girls left, the pair of them slept, sated, in each other's arms. Then she gave him the Van Cleef & Arpels cufflinks she had had made especially for him. Later, their favourite restaurant delivered his perfect menu, and Marla read him a poem that she had written recollecting their relationship to the rhythm of 'Thanks for the Memory'. They ate their meal watching an erotic video of themselves making love, which he had filmed on one of their trips. After a long, hot scented bath, she produced a box full of sex toys with which they played until they could play no more . . . and the champagne flowed, Charles Aznavour sang and time stood still. If she could have died in his arms that night, she would have willingly. But their time together was running out. Egged on by a sharp-witted and envious friend, Emil's wife was having him followed and a dossier was building up to which she added daily. She hit him with it when she was ready and, despite being torn apart, Emil buckled under her impossible demands. The house, the business, the children, the flat in Cannes, the chalet in Gstaad, did he want to lose all that, she reasoned, for the sake of what exactly? A fleeting fuck? He called Marla and said they must cool it, and not to call him, nor come in to work. The conversation was short, with little explanation, but Marla guessed immediately what must have happened. She was distraught, offended, and very, very scared. She did not hear from him for two weeks, an agonising fourteen days and nights when she fretted over the significance and magnitude of their affair in the context of her life: he loved her, she knew he did, he could not possibly give her up. But she did not dare contact him. It was inconceivable to think that it was over, that he could *abandon their love for that twitchy little woman who happened to bear his name. Then one morning, her doorbell rang and a leather-clad courier handed her an envelope. She tore it open but it contained nothing . . . except a cheque for £50,000 . . . the pay-off for her shattered heart . . .*

Annabel's Story

Annabel was twenty-one when she started a new job at an ad agency. The boss was thirty-nine, married with two children, attractive, rich and successful. Although subtle in his approach, he made it clear to Annabel that he fancied her. She had just finished with her boyfriend and was feeling half vulnerable and half ready for a fling. A dozen red roses appeared on her desk one morning with an anonymous invitation to dinner. Flattered and excited, she accepted and ended the evening being seduced in the Presidential Suite of a posh hotel in Mayfair. Annabel's head was soon turned by the promise of the good life and she soon fancied herself madly in love with her boss. Within one month she had left her parents' home and been set up in a four-storey house in Hyde Park. A gold American Express Card and a brand new BMW soon followed. Annabel had no doubt that her lover would leave his wife and in time he did, but his divorce was a long-drawn-out financially-draining affair, and the promised marriage to her never quite materialised. The years that followed were filled with domestic luxury, expensive holidays, often with his children, and a generous allowance, but Annabel became obsessed with what she did not have − a wedding ring. As she approached thirty, her demands became more insistent and a shift began to take place. Robert appeared distant, travelled endlessly on business, and adamantly refused to discuss marriage or starting a family of their own. To appease her, he bought Annabel a wild lynx coat (it was the eighties) and had her initials with his surname embroidered into the lining. She took this as a sign that her name change was imminent, but the opposite happened. Robert was having another affair and, within weeks, Annabel's comfortable lifestyle began to fall apart. He moved her out of the home they had shared into a small basement flat, cancelled her credit cards and rescinded all financial support. She tried to fight him but to no avail and had no alternative but to find a job and recommence the climb up the career ladder. Annabel is childless and still single, having missed the marital boat in her twenties, and although self-sufficient and successful, she gave the best years of her life to a man who ultimately threw them back in her face.

Trying to find 'mistress' case histories with happy endings is like looking for one particular star in the great black arch of the firmament. The very nature of the mistress/master liaison is defined by its impermanence. The moment you take away the infrequency and add quotidian routine you lose the piquancy of the situation. The cachet of not getting your heart's desire is far more seductive than getting it, which leaves you anti-climactically with nothing to strive for. Although some mistresses do get their man eventually, the honeymoon period is soon over. Once he has become the husband she always thought she wanted, she can never really trust him, and he tends to start looking for another mistress. The sexual pattern repeats itself. The urgency, expectation and passionate longing to be together is soon taken for granted and both parties find that they have lost the impetus that drove the relationship because it is now available to them all the time. This is human nature at its most contrary. Infidelity and deception may be classed as deadly sins, but they sure do keep the sexual juices flowing.

The only 'happy' ending I have found was one where the amorous couple finally extricated themselves from their significant others and got married, only for him to die shortly after. Well, at least she became his widow and not the mysterious grieving woman in the black veil standing slightly apart from the crowd at the funeral. 'Tis better to have loved and lost . . .

'Does my charisma look big in this?'

6

Body and Soul

Maggi Russell

Everybody needs a bosom for a pillow . . .

(Cornershop)

Body

From the inside looking out, we may not think that we have changed much since we were thirty, and the face we offer to the world still expresses our inner sweet bird of youth. But the day inevitably arrives when we bump into ourselves unexpectedly, perhaps encountered in a public mirror, and in that nano-second before recognition dawns, one is afforded an opportunity for objectivity. Who is that whey-faced, dumpy woman? Why is she staring at me with that tragic, tense expression? She looks vaguely familiar . . . Oh my God! *It's me!* It's my parallel universe doppelgänger, come back from the future, to warn of a wasting disease if I don't change my ways . . . but no, there can be no avoidance – it is me, *today*. A Lucien Freud representation of me, or a Dorian Gray in reverse. My true self may remain a young and fluffy chick, but my flesh betrays the turkey wattles of time.

This is not at all the way I see myself in my inner movie. This is not how I project myself up there, in my little starring cameos, on my inner eyelid fantasy screen. ME walking into the restaurant to meet HIM. Me at a party, dressed in purple velvet. Me on holiday, at a beachside café. That ME is unlined, golden, slender, fresh. But what you are actually seeing in this moment of uncalled-for honesty, is all the stress and heartbreak of your life, painted in hues of blue, with dappled grey and mauvish shadows. But take heart, for this is what everyone else actually looks like, too, when they are not posing, not attractively backlit, haven't spent two hours in hair and make-up.

When unfortunate celebrities are caught by paparazzi, out shopping in shapeless shell suits and sporting plastic carriers, they too have flat, unwashed hair, sagging chins, eyebags and grim expressions. They wail about the intrusion of telephoto lenses, but it's not really the 'lack of privacy' they object to. It's the not having time to get properly prepared. It's the having their cellulite and paunches picked out in total-surround neon sunlight. Take Jerry Hall. She seems to be two totally separate individuals masquerading as one. Jerry – all succulent lips and spun-gold tresses in the photographer's studio, but a mangy-maned centaur-woman when featured in the tabloids shouting at her kids on Caribbean beaches. In reality, she doesn't look like either of these manifestations, but is a striking older woman.

Most urban humans, without the necessary hours of grooming and lighting, look uncoordinated, unkempt, self-absorbed, depressed. Even models look like this at 9 a.m. in the studio, and couldn't possibly face the cameras until at least noon. The would-be photogenic learn that it takes a great deal of surgical intervention to look good on film, and the price is the face of an alien in real-life (Joan Rivers! Need I say more?). Adult human flesh needs an awful lot of help to look as smooth as a toddler's, arguably the only brief years when true beauty is manifest.

Of course, we don't notice this in those we love, as we've seen them looking gorgeous as many times as we've seen them looking rough. We carry a mental image of them stored in our photo memories, and having initially decided whether or not we found them attractive, that is how we continue to picture them, regardless of the effects of time. It's only when meeting someone new, without any preconceptions, that we see them untainted. Thus, if you fancied someone straight off, you probably will continue to do so, whether they age or not.

People like to say that as you age you get the face you deserve. That's a little harsh. (Though true, perhaps, for Brigitte Bardot, after all that right-wing neo-nazi stuff, plus preferring animals to people. And has Deneuve (the nerve!) really been so impeccable she has the right to retain the looks of an archangel?) Perhaps what you really get is a road map of a face – a topography of everywhere you've been, and everything you've been through (complete with spider junctions and arterial roads). Facing the truth about physical ageing can be a tough chop to chew on, and it takes a lot of courage to swallow it down. It's a bit like looking Medusa square in the face and not flinching, instead of guardedly in your shield, where the lighting is, of course, attractively dim. Perhaps we can take comfort in the thought that even Kate Moss is headed this way, and her public mirror moment will surely come. The young live for today because the future is too vast a continent, and too far off across the sea to contemplate. Now, on a clear day, you can see the coastline, and a ferry will get you there before you know it. All you can do is gamble as you travel, and take copious advantage of the duty-free bar. You know for sure you're not going to get any juicier, and today's Rock 'n' Roll is tomorrow's Rest and Recuperation. In fact, whatever you look like now, is probably the prettiest that you'll ever look again.

As we age, the hardest to pass up of all life's free gifts is beauty, and the more beautiful you have been, the more grievous the loss. Beauty as a concept in women means dewy, unlined skin, glossy hair, full lips, full breasts, flat stomach, slim hips, shapely legs, and small hands and feet. You may never have had *all* these attributes in your youth, but undoubtedly you had some of them. And you relied on them as an integral part of your female power. Now, what was bright is faded, what was sharp is soft, what was moist is dry, what was round is oval. And yet – look again. Perfect grooming and a radiant smile, graceful carriage and a knowing style, this woman has beauty too. There is elegance and individuality, nurtured out of years of intelligence and taste. Yes, she definitely has beauty, there is no other word that fits. Pshaw to pretty! This is on a higher plane, it hints at the feminine eternal.

With many women in their fifties nowadays, it is quite impossible to tell how old they really are. One twenty-four-year-old male tells me that over forty, women are regarded as pretty much the same hot potato, i.e. Attractive Older Women. Individual males either fancy going for the older option or they don't. Those who do are perfectly happy that what they see is what they get. They're not going to go off you in strong sunlight, or when they see your birth certificate. They know you're older, because you look it. That's what they like about you. (It's very heartening to learn that Johnny Rotten is married to a woman of sixty.)

The quality of beauty that is present in nubile women (and arguably they all have this by virtue of youth itself possessing magical material) is angelic, but empty. Their beauty is not there by achievement, soulfulness, intellect or effort. They have simply been lucky in their genes. They could be right little bitches, thick as wet cement, but still seductively smooth in their blank surfaces, untainted by footprints or lewd inscriptions, before they eventually dry out. Media beauty ideals demand computer-generated symmetry and baby-like proportions (big head, cute round features, long veinless limbs, delicate bones, velvet skin, silken hair). We are programmed to find all infants delicious, and people who retain these characteristics have our unconscious adoration. We automatically choose symmetrical partners with whom to have babies, and avoid the lop-sided as indicating incipient disease. Film stars have the genetic capability to retain retarded baby features into indecent adulthood, and thus look fantastic with their faces magnified fifty times. They win Oscars for their pores.

The ageing body cannot tap into this societal reservoir of unconditional love. If a woman's older, she must earn admiration and praise, if not to be overlooked for the blank babe loitering behind her. Sad men never grow out of their lust for baby flesh – a bit of the paedophile lurks in them all, although most are far too civilised to succumb. Our unconscious reaction to older women is as to our mothers. An immediate no-no as a love object to those anxious to sow and grow some seed. A yes-yes, though, to men who have always found mothers attractive (perhaps particularly their own). In the complicated human psyche, who is to say this attraction is any the more perverse?

We know that sex is not just about procreation, because during most of the times we indulge, offspring is the very last outcome we are looking for. Sex is about connection – plugging in to the universe via another person who, in the act of love, embodies the entirety of all that is not you – the mysterious, unknowable 'Other'. Perfect physical beauty does not have to be present for the experience of this ultimate satisfaction. It can be experienced ecstatically with an older woman, and has the added bonus of not putting any more strain on this over-populated world.

An older woman's beauty does not reside solely in her looks, then, but in her generous spirit, her wisdom, experience and warm sexuality. The fact that these mature qualities are not admired in a youth-obsessed media-manipulated culture does not mean they don't have potent effect in real life. At mid-life a woman's real beauty comes into its own. She now has complexity and generosity – she can give more because she is no longer obsessed with her own reflection. Narcissus has left the pool and retired to a sun-lounger to read 'Women Who Love Their Make-up Too Much'. Many men will vouch that what is lost in firm flesh is gained in the warmth and depth of the experience with an older woman. Both Cleopatra and the Queen of Sheba had the capacity to enslave, and neither were in the first flush of youth (more the hot flush of age). Madame de Pompadour had to give up on sex with Louis XV because she suffered from terrible thrush – but she still remained top of the pomps at the palace until she expired in her fifties, no doubt in a bout of ennui after so much shopping. So let's separate the bright light of truth about beauty from all the moonshine.

The beautiful older woman takes care of her body with devotional attention. Not out of overweening vanity and self-regard, but because she has finally come to realise what a miraculous gift the body is. The abuses of the past stop now. A carefully tended mature body will respond with many of the virtues of youth – vitality, energy, clear skin, good muscle tone. From now until death your body is going to need a couple of hours a day of maintenance, and tons and tons of cream. (How much natural oil do young bodies have, for heaven's sake? The skin is so thirsty, five quid's worth sinks without trace in seconds, they must have a veritable oil rig pumping away in there.) Feet, hands, elbows, knees, slather it everywhere, singing 'See you later, Alligator' as you temporarily erase the cracks, because 'After a while, Crocodile' always comes back as the sinister response.

Even easier than this continuous French polishing, is the ability to undo years of neglect. A youthful shape can be

Body and Soul

regained at any age. Scientists have discovered that muscles
keep snapping back into shape even into our eighties.
Beautiful, expensive underwear will do the rest – the
elegant older woman wears lovely lingerie every day, and
does not give in to wincyette at night. (In fact, she wears a
beautiful bra in bed, just like *Sex and The City* and porn stars,
in order to minimise chest skin stretching.) Manicures,
pedicures, haircuts, skincare, wholesome eating, moderate
exercise – all these things now become factored into her day,
as important as any other feature of her life. Seems like too
much hard work? The rewards are immense, i.e. constant
self-esteem. Are you thinking this is just for bimbos, and
intellectuals are supposed to look like Iris Murdoch? Surely
if anyone could have benefited from a makeover it was her.
If you have a brain like a planet, how can it hurt to cover the
landscape in flowers? After all, there is nothing so gorgeous
as nature, and plants don't even know how exquisite they
are. They do it because it's part of their mysterious purpose.
See beauty as your hobby, no matter how serious your
thought patterns. If an older woman looks like the wreck of
the *Mary Rose*, it's simply out of neglect. Like any sunken
ship, she's ripe for reconstruction.

There is something that fascinates about the perfectly
groomed older woman. There is mystery in her rituals, as if
she's paying homage to the goddess herself. Style and good
grooming are sexy in themselves, they suggest a woman
who revels in her own physicality, like a lesbian attracted to
herself. This is very sexy to others too, who want to find out
what all the fuss is about.

The qualities of the maturely beautiful woman then, are
animation, intelligence, self-respect, warmth, cool, presence,
charisma, control.

She can have sex with humour, or she can make of it
almost a religious ritual. Male friends, discussing this, say if
only young women were the same, life would be heaven.

151

Well, they're not and never will be, because they need commitment, and they are offering sole access to their fertility in exchange. Why should such a precious gift be offered for nothing? Young women often don't place enough value on this priceless aspect of themselves. Young men would all act like gentlemen if they had to, if that was the only way to get sex. But they don't have to. They can act like pigs, and still get laid. Women are here to train and civilise men, who without this, rapidly degenerate into beasts. Instead of playing Beauty, Girl-lads become beasts too, and single life becomes a farmyard. The older woman, having no fertility to give, can offer just the pleasures of sex (although, if she has any sense she doesn't, because the woman who offers sex without commitment has no bargaining tool at any age). Men are on their best behaviour while pursuing sex. Once they've had it, the woman is no longer a prize, but a mortal who can be had. And Beauty gets sent back home from the castle without the Prince.

Our gorgeous older woman, if she is sensible, will not even think of shacking up with anyone but the most companionable of men to enjoy her autumn afternoons with, but only when she's good and ready – maybe after sixty. Venus is in the mid-heaven and wants to play with the stars. Repressed throughout childrearing, the goddess of sex and beauty reappears in mid-life and demands her due: nymphomania, kleptomania *or* the habitual wearing of twinsets and Clarks lace-ups occur if she is not paid proper homage.

Of course, we wouldn't patronise you with so much as a hint of actual beauty advice here, there being no woman alive on the planet who doesn't already know the calorie content of the kumquat, the difference between UVA and UVB, the pros and cons of every surgical procedure from rhino- to labioplasty, and all the fiendishly clever products that improve the appearance of fine lines, thin hair, uneven pigment, love handles etc., etc., etc.

What is infinitely more interesting is whether you are *deliberately* ignoring all this, remaining oblivious to beauty routines and eating doughnuts on a regular basis. If so, what exactly is your motivation for *not* beautifying? Many of us neglect ourselves on purpose, or do ourselves intentional physical damage by over-eating, smoking, drinking and refusing to exercise. The sofa-womb becomes a place of constant retreat – as foetus-like we curl up upon it, intravenously taking in sweet creamy nutrients. This is at the very heart of bad body image, not loving your corporeal self, not paying it due respect. Why do we have such a strange, unconscious urge to do this – especially when depressed, let down, disappointed, unloved?

The soundest theory about excess weight that I have ever encountered is that it is actually displaced sadness and, more often, anger. Many of we women are very, very angry indeed, consciously or, more likely, not. We are angry at the way the media represent us, at the way men treat us, how we are not properly valued as mothers, advertising doesn't respect us, our children take us for granted and how other women can be so traitorous, especially when competing for men.

We are also very, very hungry. For anything and every- thing but food. For love, adventure, stimulation, affection, recognition, harmony, peace. These things are all hard to come by, so it's easier just to substitute iced buns.

I (MR) know all about this, because I frequently fall into this pit myself. (Wendy always looks immaculate – even when half-dead with food poisoning.) I can look seriously bad. And it's all done on purpose. For example, a man I am seeing forgets my birthday = three double choc chip muffins + one carton Ben and Jerry's Phishfood + one packet Jaffa Cakes + half a bottle of Bailey's. Result: feel too sick to even think, let alone mope. Stood up for date on Saturday night = one take-away chicken tikka masala + one peshwari naan + one matter paneer + one box Black Magic + six large rum and cokes. Result: bloated stomach, which makes whole body shape go out of wack. Consequence: lie on sofa for two days + don't wash hair or shower + only fitting outfit is ratty sweater and shapeless trackies. Result: hate self sufficiently that anger is displaced from deserving target on to self + don't say a word of complaint to real culprit, but am nice as usual + feel grateful that he wants to see me again at all 'cause I look and feel too awful for anyone else to date. Final result: VICIOUS CIRCLE.

All you slim, self-disciplined women out there may not know what I'm talking about. But I suspect you do (Pat, are you listening? Slim, gorgeous, beautifully groomed, and smokes like a fishmonger). Smoking is just a death wish disguised as sophistication. Women often say they smoke because if they didn't they'd have a huge arse. So move to Tonga – and *stay alive.*

If you're not adoring your body on a daily basis, nurturing it, feeding it tasty titbits, rubbing it with precious unguents, dressing it up in only the prettiest clothes – it's a safe bet you are angry with it. Poor sad, lonely body bearing the brunt of your vengeful mind. Of course, we can't go around machine-gunning people who hurt us, it would be a blood bath every single day. But turning it inwards is hurting the wrong guy. Better to break the chain of command, remove your own body from the line of fire, and direct the anger onto something else. Replace the ingestion of junk with the acquisition of treasure – go out and buy the £500 sheepskin coat from Maxmara. If you really can't afford it, so much the better. As you sink into debt, the true cost of your self-hatred will become evident to you. We are beside ourselves with rage, and the nearest body to hurt is our own. Turn in the other direction, away from your own form and towards something else out there in the world. Women are so used to redirecting emotions to the wrong address, like bored postal workers. We are afraid to acknowledge rage, because it smacks of the underbelly – the shadow side, the evil, black portion of our natures. Men display theirs readily enough, perhaps in a contretemps at the corner shop. We have been brought up to believe that women can't be dark, evil and violent and retain attractiveness (except perhaps dressed in furs like Cruella De Vil.) It's easier, it's lazier, it's less scary, to hold it inside rather than pushing it out. Food needs to be piled on top of it, to keep it down, like heavy weights. But rage is your body's greatest enemy, so out it must go.

Ten Steps To Ridding Yourself Of Rage
1. Feel it, own it, roll it around, bounce it up and down, exult in it – it's part of your power and your human inheritance.
2. Now direct it out and away from your own body.
3. Find a way of doing this that doesn't feel dangerous to you. (Your particular way will be uniquely suited to your own twisted black heart.)
4. It may well be something you need to do alone at home, as it feels too risky to go and do anything out in the world while angry (so no mowing men down on zebra crossings or picking them off with a rifle from tall buildings).
5. Best possible recommended way – give serious grief to the person you are angry with. Just tell them. Rant until you run out of breath. Repeatedly slam those verbal doors.
6. Can't bear to do that? Then write them a sensationally stinking letter or e-mail. Use every ugly little word you can think of. Make up new, disgusting combinations. Then (as Gustave Flaubert was advised, in pre-Madame Bovary days, by a so-called friend to whom he was reading his first unpublished novel) throw it on the fire and never speak of it again.

7. Go out into the garden and yank up weeds, imagining they are penises.
8. Get boxing gloves and a punch bag and beat the crap out of it (pummelling cushions just looks pathetic).
9. Find someone to teach you the Papua New Guinean Dance of Death. (A little ad in your local newsagent's?) Get naked, streak yourself with paint, get a spear and a drum, stamp and wail and shake your weapons, while chanting guttural death threats.
10. Take up the esoteric black arts. Burn a black candle, make an effigy of the hated one and stick pins up his dick.

All of this shocking behaviour will leave you satiated rather than sick, your stomach gratifyingly rumbly and flat, and in need of a simple nutritious snack such as a glass of wine and some peanuts, thus restoring you to the land of sunlight and Teletubbies.

WHAT THE BODY LOSES (so get over it)
Youthfulness
Stereotypical beauty ideals
Random male lust
The ability to get away with slutty clothes
Boundless energy
Fertility

WHAT THE SOUL GAINS (so get on with it)
Wisdom
Charisma
Respect
Ability to Love
Increased opportunities to laugh
Spiritual depth

Let's look at these more closely.

Youthfulness

In truth, many young women do not look so great anyway, despite having youth on their side. Many really are quite plain, and just as many are overweight. On the plus side, these will suffer less later in life through the loss of looks, than those who had beauty, and thought it was going to be all they'd ever need. Tsk, tsk, lazy girls! Skin can actually *improve* with age – big oily pores fine down and acne clears up. If I had a quid for every time a man has told me he finds fine lines sexy and attractive, I would have enough to buy a pot of night cream made from calf foetuses and snail slime (I'm not kidding). Getting rid of lines doesn't really work anyway, and botox is a grisly idea, bringing on a kind of botulism of the muscles, and the more you have it done the more your face will resemble the features of the moon – only instead of the Sea of Tranquillity it will be the Desert of Desolation. Welcome to Deadpan Alley.

Stereotypical beauty ideals

The current beauty ideal, slim but with big breasts, is not realistic even for young women. We could cry over the way our gorgeous daughters agonise about the slightest sign of fat, the shape of their legs and chests, rounded stomach etc., etc. The intelligent thing to do, rather than rushing out for breast implants and liposuction, is to stop and think about what beauty ideals signify in the culture at large, rather than feeling one has to conform. We all know the theory that in times of famine fat is prized, in times of plenty thin is in. Tits are now a fashion item, and a safe area for sexual signification, so thin woman, big tits means: young, culturally acceptable, safely sexy. Thanks to Jennifer Lopez and all those fit black girls parading the High Streets in little more than thongs, the big bum has also broken out of the concentration camp, and taken over as erogenous zone number one. The vagina will never become a high-fashion area because men are just too terrified of it – especially gay men, who do all the designing. Most women too, come to that, because we all came out of one of these alarmingly tiny Tardis-type receptacles, which when you think about it, is a totally mad idea. Only lesbians and midwives are nonchalant about them. So areas of the body will always go in and out of fashion, each a fetishised alternative to the pudenda, which will remain the sacred and profane forbidden city. The only way to go is to make the most of your body type, dress it up accordingly, adore it unconditionally, and wait for men who like your kind, of which there will be many. Don't listen to women who want to see you starve yourself into a stereotype like them. Just forbid them to talk to you that way. As the human race advances, great gains are made, but also great losses. Thus one day, when we can clone perfect people, everyone will physically fit the stereotype. This will mean we lose fascinating diversity, and good-looking people will hate this, because no longer will they have this unfair advantage over rivals. Ugly people will, of course, do nothing but welcome this, as to go through life unpretty is an unpleasant burden.

Random male lust

Being constantly leered at and propositioned on the street – well, was that really so great? Of course, none of us really appreciated this until it had completely ceased, and then we lamented its passing. (Or is it just that men are more politically correct these days?) Chaps bellowing 'I love you' out of passing cars, 'Hallo gorgeous' as a cacophony that accompanied your passage, being followed for miles by strangers, the muttering of obscenities by Egyptians on the Edgware Road, cars parked outside your house for hours, stalkers with binoculars trained on your bedroom window – all this glorious attention we took for granted, and then one day we went out on to the street and heard the pins dropping. It is as if you are not there, and it is all pavement people can do to walk around and not through your transparent body. But all that has happened is that you have joined the rest of the human race, who go about their business unimpeded, unremarked upon, unseen. You can now sit on the tube without men undressing you, that thing poking in your back as you strap-hang IS a rolled-up newspaper, your perfume will not inflame on the escalator. After the shock of this wears off you realise this is no bad thing. The leering of men may have given you a frequent adrenaline boost, you thought it made you powerful, but actually it weakened you, that power was an illusion. It made you an object for others to pick up or discard. And all those dates you had – honestly, how many of them were actually worth having? Have you really had more meaningful relationships than your plainer friends? You can forget that paralysing youthful self-consciousness too, today you are free to both walk and think. Now, in your movements around Waitrose you are like a mysterious ninja; invisible, swift, silent, and deadly purposeful.

The ability to get away with slutty clothes

This is one for the ladies in Kilroy's studio audiences. Whenever his researchers are doing an over-forties 'Growing Old Disgracefully' show, no doubt they phone up prospective candidates and say, 'Now please be sure to run out and buy a cropped top to show, no doubt off your midriff (mid-drift?) or something see-through and a black wonderbra, a miniskirt in something shiny, red high heels, and maybe a wig and masses of make-up. Kilroy will love you'. Many of these items look slutty enough on young women, who should also know better. Breasts, thighs, navels, bottoms – these are fine on the beach, or any body-shop type activity where everyone else is semi-naked too. But on the urban street, it's asking for trouble, and looks like touting for trade. At any age. On older women it looks so much the worse, by incremental stages, as the years increase. It just should never happen in daylight hours. If you have a fabulous body, you can still show this off in close-fitting garments that skim your curves, in touch-me fabrics. Anything skin-tight, low-cut or cutaway, should be cut right out. Please burn all offending items now, and don't even think of giving them to Oxfam, as innocent fools might snap them up and look even cheaper and get into even more trouble wearing them than you did. (Donate some of those nice practical sweaters instead.) Middle-aged men, of course, look just as bad, with their inappropriate ponytails and cowboy boots. They can just about get away with these, I suppose, if they're being ironic and doing reunion gigs with their rock band, but generally the White Quiffs of Dover should carry danger signs about going right over the top.

Boundless energy
I don't know about you, but I (MR) never had this when young, anyway. I always preferred to sleep till noon at the very least, and followed the maxim: never stand up if you can sit, never sit if you can lie down, and never lie down if you can lose consciousness completely. Narcoleptics have always provoked my envy, as they have somehow wangled permission to fall asleep suddenly, anywhere, anytime, whenever things get boring. It seems to me that lots of older women (Wendy!) have much more energy than most young women, and get so much done in a day it makes lazy girls like me dizzy. As long as you have enough energy to do the minimum required to keep your shit going, let it be enough. Arguably, most people are all doing far too much, anyway, and less being done would be a blessing all round. Let's start a movement to slow the world right down. From now

on, do everything at the most leisurely pace possible; take two hours for lunch, have a siesta, gossip on the phone, soak your feet in peppermint foot balm, watch soaps, and only do a little work if you absolutely must, to pay rent or something. Please don't make a virtue of all your manic rushing around. Just give up. You know it makes sense, and you'll always have time for a laugh and to notice the goddess of the small things that make this life worthwhile.

Fertility

This I have left to last, because arguably it is the one huge thing that you have undeniably lost, and nothing else is comparable to. That said, of course lots of us give this up with relief, and even the hormones that go with it are a joy to see the back of as they pack up and troop off to Florida. Others find this hard, because it's such a swansong – where have all my periods gone? If I'm grumpy (all the time) now, how can I blame it on PMT? Am I in Permanent Maladjusted Turmoil? Has happiness forever fled? Psychologically, no longer being fertile undoubtedly detracts from our store of womanliness, and a feeling of impending androgyny flutters like an ugly moth on the edge of consciousness. But meditating on the end of fertility will reap more benefit than trying to ignore it. Read Christiane Northrup's biblical epic *The Wisdom of The Menopause* to get a clear perspective on this, including the HRT debate. Personally, I prefer not to go the chemical route because I don't want to be kept on an artificial hormone life-support machine. If my ovaries want to close down the factory and retire, then I think they've deserved their pension. My womb revolts against this New Labourite plan to make it go on working until it's seventy, and for no useful purpose, as no more eggs are actually going to get delivered. That said, I take every herbal remedy I can get my hands on to relieve weird symptoms such as sudden spontaneous combustion (hot flushes), *The Blair*

Witch Project soundtrack (racing heart beat), and sudden overwhelming premonitions of impending doom while queuing in the Post Office (oestrogen dips). When fertile, all those other subconscious crazinesses had control of you – absolute, uncalled for necessity of shagging, mainlining chocolate, losing control during sex and then remembering it a fraction too late, regular DIY pregnancy tests while praying not to get pink spots or blue circles, and, finally, unintentional single parenthood. Serenity comes when fertility goes. You don't have to compulsively go out and hunt down monsters to have sex with every Saturday night, you can choose instead to spend your time with nice girlfriends, secure that your eggs are not staging a secret passing out parade, leading your psyche up the garden path and into the badlands where dragons lurk. The end of fertility unleashes vast changes in the psyche, releasing a great deal of contingent energy, *Chi, prana* or whatever you want to call it, freeing it up for more consciously directed activities. And so it comes to pass, that what the body loses, the soul unquestionably gains.

Soul

The soul seems to be this year's must-have fashion accessory, like beaded handbags last season, and pashminas the year before. Nowadays, everyone wants one, and no doubt there are marketing men holding meetings right now, trying to figure out how they are going to persuade you to buy one in every colour, just like they've succeeded with the concept of cool. Cool was originally a defence against pain and humiliation, the province of a courageous black community who shut their ears to white death threats with noisy jazz music, protected their minds through copious amounts of weed, and cut out ugly sights by wearing groovy shades and low-brimmed hats even in bed. The way that privileged white kids now describe everything as 'kewl' is pathetic, nauseating, sheep-like and moronic, depending as it does on purchasing the right mobile phones, trainers, jeans, etc., from only the 'right' emporia, and at vastly inflated prices. The soul is the next big happening marketing opportunity, so be on your guard. You have been warned. Soulful cars, couches, can-openers, they're all making their way into a catalogue near you.

Everyone can claim to have a soul, all you need to do is believe in the theory. No-one has actually ever seen one, and some people that one meets unquestionably do not have one at all. Buildings either sing of it in every brick (old theatres and churches) or groan their lack of it (national car parks). Descriptions of the soul range from the spiritual channel of the Great Creator, to the meaning of that funny feeling like indigestion in your gut, and our dreams are believed to be the language of its communication. A general rule seems to be that when one is very busy, with no time to look within, the soul goes to sleep. But ignored for too long, it will act up, throw a wobbler, and toss your car off a bridge. Looking after a family, productive and useful as this has been, has meant putting masses of energy into other people, leaving no time for your Self. This can leave you with an exhausted and hollow feeling, out of touch with your inner truth, your soul.

There is a lexicon of clichés about the soul. One thing is for sure, it's not a question of candles, feng shui, macro-biotics or yoga. It is more to do with keeping in constant touch with your intuition, following your gut feelings, knowing instinctively what is right – all things that prove women are naturally much more soulful than men. Effeminate is a pejorative term, and yet should be a state to aim at, meaning as it does instinct, feeling, intuition, emotion and depth. Soul is irrational, moody, unpredictable. (In that case PMT can surely be claimed as a manifestation of soul.)

When events are following a logical plan the soul nods off, just like the sun in the day blots out the moon and stars. Dreams don't seem relevant at these times, we don't remember them on waking, or pay them only scant attention. But in the dark nights of psychological crisis, the voice of the soul emerges, and strange images and ideas take a grip of our sleeping and waking hours. We act out of character, we are contrary, we feel drawn by strange desires.

By mid-life we have usually settled into familiar psychological and social patterns, ensconced in work and family, and we think we know who we are. Then suddenly, a crisis occurs, you wake up from the torpor of your life, and everything has gone topsy-turvy. A new and pressing urge has come upon you, to change your ways, to seize the day, to walk out the door and stand naked in the rain. You are a threat to the established order around you. And your soul is the source of this renegade, inventive force.

The soul at mid-life often cannot be contained. It demands to be seen and honoured, and it can be fearsome in its insistence to be heard. Sometimes it is terrifying in its force. It will smash up families, marriages and careers. It doesn't care how uncomfortable it makes you, or who else in your life it hurts. Thus husbands at mid-life take up with bimbos and buy yachts in the Caribbean, wives walk out on twenty-five years of wedded bliss in Woking to marry Maori tribesmen, or join Inuit communes and take up throat singing.

Hermes is the mythological god of passage from one dimension to another, the guardian of doorways. In the withering away of the old life, and the birth of the new, he can be called upon as your guide (and I don't mean just go out and buy the headscarf).

The more we have entrenched ourselves in mental attitudes and social positions, the more we overlook the fact that goals have been attained at the cost of stunting our growth. Choosing one path rules out others, and passions once held dear have had to be given up. Depression increases in people over forty. Rather than a source of fear, this could be interpreted as a major change underway in the psyche, something repressed rising in the soul. It may be the rediscovery of something forgotten since childhood, or the yearning for experience that is entirely new. Current preoccupations may suddenly lose their bite. The deaths of parents in particular can bring on this change, because as long as you have at least one parent, a part of you is still a child. Sacrifices and losses are not as disastrous as they at first appear – they leave room for new and animated experiences to enter.

Depression at mid-life, coming along hand in hand with the menopause, feeling like a kind of death at the time, actually allows the birth of something fresh and new. A second chance, a second coming, the opportunity finally to express your own unique soul in the world, a soul that has been lobotomised by the previous pressures of your life. It's time to bury your fertility, your mother-role, and your domestic goddess image of self. Let these act as fertiliser for the tree that is emerging, one that will bear the strange fruit of new creative endeavours, new adventures, new passions, or parts of yourself that you have been pruning back. Look forward now to everything you are about to gain.

Wisdom

All those crazy irresponsible acts of youth are far behind you now. Young people are forgiven the first time they do wrong, the second time they go to prison. Some mid-life people, like rehab inmates let loose in a night-club, make foolish choices in the heady rush to wreck their own lives. You now know better about lots of things, like sleeping with friends' (or children's!) husbands, stealing other people's thunder (Raquel Welch, shame on you for ruining your daughter-in-law's wedding by turning up in a low cut mini-dress), upstaging friends at their parties, grabbing all the available attention, being needy, arrogant, selfish, vain – all the things that aren't attractive in the young, but are so prevalent, because they are still intent on building (necessarily) strong egos and discovering the limits of their own gifts and personalities. Nor do you need to experiment with drugs, emotions, lesbianism, swinging, leather. You've reached a stage where you've done all the lab work, got your results, written the report and it's all filed away. You have been through all this, you have reached a point where you know yourself pretty well, you are ready to move up to the next stage, the transpersonal phase, in which spiritual awareness is coming closer to you every hour of every single day. Instead of grabbing everything you can for yourself, you are more intent on helping improve life situations for others, the holistic view that all humanity is One, and the day you meet your creator is now on the calendar.

Charisma
You now possess a certain warm, radiant, drawing-eyes quality. People listen when you speak, their eyes soften when they look at you. Knowing yourself so well now, you can unwind, be yourself, unpretentious, honest, truthful, self-deprecating, but aware of your own worth. This is as potent as beauty. People may not so much want to shag you, as to be near you, and drink up your presence. You make them feel good, relaxed, comfortable, valued. It's a force of love, worth more than all the supermodel glamour in the world.

Respect
Your calmness, stillness, grace and quiet authority (but do retain the dirty laugh) command respect in young and old alike. To insult you would be a crass act, rebounding on the perpetrator. A sure way to ensure respect is to avoid taking

anything other people say or do personally. That rude cow who pushed ahead of you in the supermarket, the road rage, the jostling on the tube, being ignored in shops – bide your time, hum a little tune, and meanwhile try to imagine what it is actually like to work on a till and have to deal with the public. These people are in a living hell. You are a free spirit, dropping in to pick up some charcoal for the barbecue, soon to be wafting away with your purchase, soon to have your feet up with a vodka and tonic, while other poor creatures will still be on shift at 9 p.m. If you must have revenge, let that be it – because others are rude their life is purgatory. Their fiery pit is not your concern – you're going back to the little arbour in heaven that you have built for yourself, and that you deserve. It was earned from all the times you kept your temper, let the insult go over your head, and didn't waste a single drop of your energy on the pettiness of others. So, next time some disrespectful bastard barges into you with a trolley, or nicks your parking space, shrug, smile, and be grateful you are not them.

Spiritual depth

People with this quality never ever discuss it, claim it, affect it or try to project it, yet everyone notices it, right away. Even pets pick up on it. It emanates from them like light and heat. Of course the Dalai Lama has it, manifest in his humility, and his sweet, sweet smile. It's a bit like sexiness, but whereas that is pheromones, this has no scent. People who are both spiritual and sexy at the same time are so inherently powerful, they could rock the world, only they choose not to. Since Jimi Hendrix, very few have actually managed to do this. Those with spiritual depth are joyful, sorrowful, self-deprecating, self-assured, serene, hilarious, bright and shadowy, all at once. Rather than other-worldly, they are as fully human as it is possible to be. As such they are a shining model of How To Live, and if you are lucky enough to have one in your social circle, treasure them and emulate everything they say and do.

The Compleat Woman

So how to be a human being with body and soul integrated and acting as one? First, be human before you are woman. The soul has no gender.

1. **Be Funny**. If you can't think of anything witty to say, just laugh a lot at others' jokes, and this will always make you popular with everyone. In particular learn to laugh at your own defeats.
2. **Be Kind, but not nice**. Nice is polite and phoney, kind is an act of sheer generosity. Most other people really need this, and it's no skin off your nose.
3. **Be Strong**. Life will test you on a daily, if not hourly, basis – be ready to face every challenge head-on and wrestle it to the ground.
4. **Don't Judge**. It's not your job. What people do or say is their own impenetrable mystery and not for you to take personally. If someone is pissing you off, just walk away.
5. **Watch what you say**. Words are weapons, and cause wars. Question everything you are about to utter. Don't say the first thing that comes in to your mind – who knows which one of your many inner demons has control at that moment? Words have power, so use them advisedly. No one knows anything, anyway, and all talk is just a little gossip in a great silence, to quote the great Danny Abse.
6. **Do Your Best At All Times**. That is all anyone can ever try to do. Whatever the situation, think: what would be the best thing for the most number of people here, and do that if you possibly can. Sometimes, some situations will be a lot easier than others. Do your best, then forget all about it. And there's no need to judge yourself if you failed.

How to be Happy at Last

The poet WH Auden wrote as illuminatingly about love and happiness as anybody, and summed up a lifetime of contemplation with the following excellent advice: just hang on to the few best moments of your life, live them over and over again, and forget all the rest. Here are some of the things to forget:

- Don't be a bitch (very nineties).
- Don't be a lady (very eighties, whether three times, in red, or laying across his big brass bed).
- Don't be a chick (very seventies).
- Don't be a bird (very sixties).
- Don't be a yardbird or a bird dog (very fifties, and so long ago that nobody knows what they were) and, of course, never be any kind of dog at all.

So what are we to call ourselves now? Not crones, earth mothers or witches. I propose a motion that our black brothers have got it right. The same culture that adopted 'ho' (whore) as an unexpected term of affection for their women, also refer to those they hold in high esteem as Big Women (refreshing as a contrast to little women, and they don't mean fat) and, even better, their *Queens*. This fit feels snug. Whether we be Queens of the Stone Age or Queens of the Space Age, we all have something in common. A Queen has to be mature and maternal. She has to rule, to be dignified, gracious and commanding in bling-bling jewellery and extravagant headgear. She needs a bosom worthy of a few medals. A Queen represents the soul on a tarot card, and also in alchemy. Soul is something that the older woman, the archetypal prehistoric Queen, embodies by virtue of her age, her wisdom and her sex, and she is holding all the cards, in hearts, diamonds, clubs and spades.

'. . . men, dates, sex, make-up, diets, botox, boob jobs, top jobs, blow jobs, dick size, men, men, men . . .'

7

The Sisterhood

Wendy Salisbury

Friends are God's apology for relations.

(Hugh Kingsmill)

If a dog is a man's best friend, what is a woman's?

(a) Full-on lycra bodywear with superfit control panels and a reinforced gusset?

(b) A box of Bendicks Bittermints delivered daily to your door?

(c) Your telephone bill paid in perpetuity by someone else?

Marilyn Monroe may have purred '. . . diamonds . . .' but a girl's best friend is, in fact, her best friend(s). No matter what life throws at us, and there are times when our heads feel like coconuts on the shy at The Great Funfair of Existence, our chances of getting by are greatly improved 'with a little help from our friends'. They are our sisters in solidarity, our advisors in adversity, our sympathetic sounding boards, our asexual soul mates, our joint seekers of truth, the keepers of our consciences and the bridges over the troubled waters we navigate as we sail the sea of life. There is a very distinctive bond that exists between women, a common empathy acquired over centuries of dealing with the kind of exclusive privileges God devised especially for us: puberty, breasts, unwanted body hair, PMT, periods, falling in love, losing your virginity, sex, birth control, rape, pregnancy, childbirth, post-natal depression, child rearing, infidelity, divorce, menopause, old age, death (well, that sucked, didn't it?). And some people say God is a woman? I don't think so. (Man's biggest problem? Getting it up and keeping it up.) The general knowledge handed down through the female line crosses continents like an international network, but in this case the www. stands for Website of Womanly Wisdom, *sisterhood.com* into whose search engine we can enter our quandary and come up with a whole series of suggestions on how to solve it.

You only have to observe a group of female friends of any age enjoying a girlie lunch or night out together and you cannot fail to notice the very unique dynamic that exists between them. As an entity, these women appear to be directly descended from the Amazons, with their confident manner, assertive attitude, excited laughter and integrated body language. Of course, this is all a sham put on for the benefit of whichever Swallows happen to be watching. We may have polish on our nails, blonde streaks in our hair and high heels on our feet, but this is just war paint – *fool the people you fear, and you fool yourself as well*. Deep down we are all little girls with grown-up anxieties, but we can brainstorm, draw strength and recharge our individual batteries from the communal power station that we generate together. Our conversations cover every topic from Accessories to Zen (and men, men, men) and our mutual interest in the politics and passions thereof are affirmed by our visual, verbal and aural interest in the minutest detail of every story our sisters have to tell. That caring, sharing, every-little-thing-that-we-are-wearing interaction denotes a unity of spirit and a spirit of unity as close-knit as chainmail, the chain only being broken by a male. (Observe a group of men in similar circumstances and the profundity of their discourse would be a muttered debate about whose round it is, followed by a reverential supping of pints while staring straight ahead at a green screen. The silence may be broken by an occasional air punch to abuse or applaud one of the little running stick figures with baggy shorts and muddy knees. And these are the people the world relies on for all the answers to all the questions . . .)

The great electrician in the sky wired us differently and our communication skills attest to that. Having a good friend is like having a separate brain in another head that we can turn on when our own mental computer flashes 'overload'. The intimate life-sharing between us is essential to our mental health and wellbeing but mystifies most men, who deny themselves and each other the finer points of their problems, thus escaping the complication of ever actually addressing an issue. I asked a male friend of mine what it was that men talked about and his immediate reply was, 'Anything that does not reveal our insecurities', including such life-reforming topics as football and (gross exaggerations about) sex. This negation of depth, honesty and sentiment means that any inarticulate oaf who's ever kicked a ball or unleashed the beast can hold court with immodest tales of machismo and sportsmanship, thus raising his profile with his fellow peers. (But you don't fool us . . .) Even with their so-called 'best mates', men would never disclose any emotional trauma, as this would be viewed as a sign of weakness. The average bloke is constantly bragging and strutting in order to kid the world and his wife that he is doing better than he actually is, and when he looks in the mirror he sees a fan-tail peacock where in fact there is only a man's pale wee cock.

Women have no qualms about denigrating themselves to their gal pals in a 'Look at the size of my arse!' kind of way. They rely on their friends to advise on every issue: career, romance, family, fashion and diet, laying bare their very souls to each other in order to rebuild and improve. We think nothing of spending an entire evening examining the re-growth on each other's inner thighs to find a quicker and cleaner way of frightening off the follicles. Whether we're moaning about our oversized tums or giggling about his undersized plums, no land is too foreign to be explored. Medical problems are a particular favourite, the monthly period being a bottomless pit of a topic with its vagaries, cubic capacity, length and consistency being heralded as in: 'Well they had to raise the Thames Barrier for mine last month, two Super Tampax and a rolled-up bath towel still couldn't staunch it.' Eeeow! Birthing stories are another boundless bonding exchange, the more complicated and painful the better. The one who pops it out and goes back to work the next day barely raises a ripple (nipple?) whereas the breach baby who was three weeks late and had to be delivered on the night of the storm by emergency caesarean on the floor of a passing meat truck after a 38-hour labour where the heartbeat was failing and the cord was twisted twice round its neck gets a much higher score on the clap-o-meter. Men exaggerate (lie) because to them the truth is too unappealing to contemplate. Imagine meeting a man who tells you that he is a street sweeper living in a workman's hut, with a one-bar fire, which backs on to the railway track at Walthamstow, but you're welcome over any time for a shag? Unless you fancied the council uniform pants off him, you'd hardly be swept away by his self-promotion. If, however, he tells you that he's just sold his latest invention to Bill Gates and would like to meet you in The Four Seasons for a glass of champagne and a niblette of caviar, your knicker elastic would be twanging before you'd even asked: *'A quelle heure?'* The one thing these gents have in common is that they both want to get their leg-over and Mr Lying Toad reckons he's in with a better chance than Mr Brutally Honest, and he's probably right. But no matter how successful they are, most men are unsure of themselves in the physical arena, due to a serious design fault that makes them vulnerable and liable to failure. Women know this and men know that we know this, hence the self-enhancement . . . but I digress . . . back to The Sisterhood.

A friend is a single soul dwelling in two bodies.

(Aristotle)

The dictionary defines the word 'friend' as 'a person known well to another and regarded with liking, affection and loyalty'. Liking and affection are easy: these are feminine attributes and can be dispensed as simply as tissues from a pop-up box. As long as the person to whom they are directed is worthy, they cost nothing and contain doses of feel-good factor for the donor. But loyalty? Now there's a generous and complicated gift. It means behaving with a pure heart, offering your unswerving support, being constant, dependable, steadfast and true. Rather like a Knight of the Round Table. Not a very female trait, with our devilish, tricksy, self-seeking ways that lead us oft into temptation. (Like that infamous night when, high on a cocktail of lust and vodka, you bonked your best friend's boyfriend because he was there and she wasn't. This is not commonplace, but it can happen and – even stranger – the female friendship can survive it. Later, comparisons and jokes may be made at the expense of the sperm donor, which only helps to strengthen the bond between the two women.)

Aristotle also described friendship as 'a mutual love of people who wish each other well', but the term is often misused, and friendship has many faces, some true, some false. True friendship is unconditional, non-judgemental, sincere and accepting. Geography may keep you apart and you may not speak nor see each other for weeks, months or even years, but that essence of understanding and integrity cannot be broken. You may only call your friend in a crisis and, if she is true, she will offer support and compassion, not compound your misery by criticism and reproach. She will listen earnestly to your recriminating rambles swinging like a metronome in beat with your moods. If it's to do with a man (and frankly, my dear, when isn't it?) she'll hate the rotten bastard when you do and love him right back again when you say it's OK. Irrespective of its magnitude, the problem will be examined in the most rigorous detail. Others will be rallied to give advice and opinion and to listen to imaginary themes, schemes, backdated texts and voice messages, drafts of e-mails and letters and more hypotheses than spirits in Heaven to try and discover precisely what he meant by: 'I need some space'. (Goodbye.) Thus, another great consolation of a circle of understanding friends is the fortune that can be saved in therapist's fees.

False friendship involves the feigning of sincerity by someone whose only intention is to stab you in the back. She probably didn't mean it because she was barking mad at the time, but I was the victim of betrayal from my closest friend over a period of many years. She cheated me out of thousands of pounds I could ill afford by pretending to have cancer. We were as close as two girls could be, sharing our homes, our children, and all our spare time. The fake illness involved a lot of 'treatment', but the money she conned out of me and others was spent on a boob job, an abortion, an eye lift, a new car and designer clothes. Her friendship was an endurance test but I loved and trusted her and she seemed so convincing . . . The emotional trauma she put me through involved asking me to help her 'end it all when the pain got too much' and to look after her children 'when she was gone'. I also spent much of my time helping her clean out and redecorate her shambolic home. She sure knew how to use me. Looking back, I can't believe I was so gullible. She was eventually sectioned by her ex-husband who did not believe her claim that she only had 'six months to live' and she subsequently spent a few weeks in a mental hospital. I think of her often and miss her still, but it was all too draining and exhausting to re-kindle.

The curative power of true friendship is as potent as a course of penicillin. If a woman has a mental or physical trauma, she will immediately phone a friend for a pain-killing injection of good sense and constructive input, after which, whether a solution has been reached or not, she will invariably feel better. The stories we women tell each other form the road maps of our lives: no turning is taboo, no terrain too tricky to tread. We will divulge our intimacies in the most delicate detail, sharing each other's agony and ecstasy with unflinching candour. (Imagine a man giving his mate a blow-by-blow account of how he was looking for the perfect pair of crotch huggers to go with his black lycra hipsters and after having trawled the length and breadth of Oxford Street finally found them in a discount bin at the back of Mr Byrite.) The stuff we impart is sensational, emotional, self-deprecating, subjective, devastating and designed to be dissected. The best, nay, the only way we can cope is to discuss, to analyse, to bemoan and finally to laugh. Our actions and reactions make us who we are and our joint memories, be they funny or sad, are the money in the banks of our beings. By reliving and relating our experiences, we affirm that we have travelled and are travelling still.

A friend and I once spent an entire afternoon reminiscing about shoes we had known and loved. The rites of passage from childhood to widowhood could be traced with every single sandal, sneaker, stiletto and slipper we recalled, for each and every footstep held a special memory: the pair of red kitten heels she wore for her fourteenth birthday party the night she got French-kissed for the first time, the pink T-straps my mother refused to buy me that I later blagged off my Dad and took to school in my satchel to show off during break, the rope-soled espadrilles from Corfu still sandy from *that night* on the beach, the lace-front thigh-length gold boots I felt like Barbarella in; these shoes were made for walking, and walk and talk they did.

Whenever a friend succeeds, a little something in me dies.

(Gore Vidal)

Girlfriends never lapse into awkward silences for there is always something crucial to discuss: to B or not to B(otox), wheat intolerance, ceramic versus metal hair straighteners, how to lose a stone by Saturday, vaginal or abdominal hysterectomies, growing bougainvillea, Pat Butcher's earrings. The serious stuff gets dealt with too, of course, and that ain't heavy if she's your sister. But standing centre stage in the full spotlight is the main topic for discussion: relationships and, of course, the begetters thereof: men. Our men, your men, their men, men we have known, loved, dated, mated, hated, thumped, dumped, forgiven, forgotten, sought and fought, it's an immutable subject and one of which we will never tire. Like the tide, it varies hourly and like the tide, we never know if we're coming or going. By sharing our triumphs and our traumas we can draw comfort from the fact that no matter the end result, the others will be there to pick up the pieces. There is communal joy at the successes, and a *frisson* of schadenfreude at the failings. Of course, we don't consciously wish anyone ill, especially not our best buddies, but it does help to ratify our own misfortunes to know that others are suffering similar fates. And to give our brains a rest from all this man management, we discuss the other issues that confront us in our daily lives: children who go off travelling and forget to phone home, aging relatives who put vinegar on their cornflakes and comb their hair with a fork, the depressing discovery of strands of silver where once there were coils of gold, the loss of oestrogen that must be replaced at any cost (wild yam, black cohosh, sex with strangers?), and the gain of testosterone as you rage irrationally at the cretin behind the counter or at the call centre.

Female friendships fall into many categories and, like shoes, you can have different ones for different occasions. There is a girl I go to the cinema with once a month. We have an enjoyable evening debating why Pacino has never had his eye bags done, what we would cook for Clooney if he ever came to dinner, and how the young blonde bitches making millions today cannot hold a candle to stars like Lana Turner and Rita Hayworth. I consider Angela a good friend but I wouldn't dream of telling her I 'entertained' my next door neighbour, who is twenty years my junior, when his girlfriend was away. I have another friend who I called the minute he left, who laughingly told me off but then demanded every detail in glorious Technicolor, yet she and I don't enjoy the same films. Another girlfriend smokes and drinks, and although I try to resist both, whenever we get together I match her fag for fag and glass for glass, until we end the evening like a pair of ashtrays talking rubbish in fluent Vodka. Siblings have their own brand of comradeship as they share not only their bloodline but also their childhood and formative years. The rivalry that exists between them is usually caused by their parents, and some fall out because they are so close that judgement and criticism of each other is actually directed at themselves. I have a wonderful sister who lives abroad and although I only see her twice a year, we are as united today as we were aged six and nine when we stayed awake throughout Christmas Eve listening intently for Santa Claus. (She knew it was Daddy, but she never let on to me.) Mothers and daughters can be the greatest of friends, though the generation and power imbalance can lead to arguments when one or the other oversteps the mark and the boundaries have to be redefined. There was a time when my two teenage daughters and I lived together and were all dating at the same time. I had to have a second phone number installed because one of us was always waiting for a call and the other two couldn't bear it when the lucky recipient spent hours hogging the line. (There were many displays of petulance and much slamming of doors, but I try not to do that so often these days because it damages my paintwork.)

Female friendships were forged through the ages by necessity as well as choice. While the men folk went off a'hunting, a'whoring and a'warring, the women stayed home and held the fort, delighted to have some peace and quiet, and time for a good old natter over a cooking pot or a spinning machine. In African tribal culture, the women were the architects of society, designing and building the mud huts, pounding the grain and baking the bread, while the men lazed around all day smoking and scratching (nothing new there, then). But this was before Llewellyn-Bowen and Jamie Oliver showed men the way. And think what the women embroidering the 230-feet long Bayeux Tapestry must have talked about, all those months and years they sat nose to nose threading their colourful wools back and forth creating the 72 scenes on the world's most ambitious piece of canvas. I bet that Norman got a right old roasting on the battle field and off, with his funny little helmet and his long thrusty sword. This bonding ritual is multiplied by women the world over, be they making honey cake to sell at summer fêtes, campaigning against weapons of mass destruction, or posing nude for calendars to raise money for leukaemia. In an ethos of community spirit, their time is metaphorically spent stitching together the pieces of the quilt that constitutes the fabric of their lives.

There is a certain hierarchy in the pecking order of friendship, and rivalries obviously exist where females group together. Be they in canvas tents or on an upmarket housing estate, there will be an Alpha female assuming the role of leader around whom the other hens revolve. Her second-in-command would be thought of as her Best Friend, a position that holds a certain amount of kudos. My cousin proved herself as such the dawn she was called and told of Alpha's mother's death in the night. She threw on a tracksuit and trainers, dragged a comb through her hair and drove straight over. As the other girls gathered later in the day, soberly dressed, discreetly made-up and neatly coiffed, the sight of Brenda in her state of 'I literally came right over . . .' confirmed the fact that she had been telephoned first and so was, indeed, the Best Friend. To be needed and heeded by our peers draws out our giving side as we gain the quiet satisfaction of the amateur counsellor advising and guiding others through their own personal quagmire and back on to solid ground. And the more we listen, the more we learn, or at least, that's the theory. Their pressures and pitfalls should serve as a warning to us, alerting us to tread our own paths more carefully, although, of course, nothing is quite as rewarding as making your own mistakes. Friends are the rocks we cling to through the shipwrecks, and the sunlight we bask in when the storms have passed. Our mutual need for, and dependence on, each other is a vital ingredient in our psychological growth as we acknowledge the true meaning of give and take. The ups, the downs, the smiles, the frowns are all endured and enjoyed in the solace of knowing that we are not alone. The ebb and flow of friendship means that sometimes you're the ship and sometimes you're the port.

The best way to find out who your real friends are is to fall flat on your face. When you count the people reaching down to help you up, you will recognise but a faithful few.

The sycophants and flatterers will quickly disappear and you don't have to be rich and famous to learn this. Some fair-weather friends will fail you miserably when put to the test, like the one who crossed the road to avoid me when she heard that my last relationship had broken up. Rather than have to give me a hug and ten minutes (OK, fifteen) of her precious time, she chose to ignore me, hoping I would go away. I did. Another long-term buddy and I fell out when she made an unacceptably critical judgement of my younger lover, in a voice so acid with the taste of sour grapes, I saw her for her true colours and decided I no longer needed her in my life. There is a certain satisfaction in dumping difficult friends, we don't always have time to see the ones whose company we enjoy, so why waste time on the jealous drainers and the selfish takers?

The basis for an enduring and solid friendship is a shared history and the joint memories attached thereto – the more complicated the history, the stronger the bond. She may have been the little girl who came up to you on the first day of school and asked if you wanted to play hopscotch. When she lent you her stone, you were overwhelmed by a feeling of trust and relief. This happens less as you grow older due to our highly-developed cynical sides, but that is not to say that true friendships cannot be forged in later life. You may walk into a crowded room full of strangers and gravitate towards someone with whom you instantly connect. The chemistry is unmistakeable as you recognise a kindred spirit. Maybe you knew each other in a previous life. You may share the same sense of humour, enjoy the same music, books, films and food, aspire to a similar lifestyle, fancy the same type of men. Sometimes it's none of these things, you just click. And it's not only about having friends – it's also about being a friend. We've all felt guilty at not keeping in touch with someone, but when we or they eventually make that call, we can slip easily into a catch-up conversation without having to lie, apologise nor pack an oversized trunk for a Jewish guilt trip.

The first childhood friend I remember was the one from the playground, though she deceived me before too long. We sat together in class, whispered during lunch, skipped all through playtime and wrote long letters from W2 to NW3 and back again every night – a proper letter with a stamp on it (2½d) which arrived daily in the morning post – what a grown-up thrill that was at seven years old. But one day I saw her writing a letter to someone else, another girl in the same class. I had no idea she was so prolific, nor could afford so many stamps. I felt utterly betrayed and ceased my confidential outpourings forthwith. To add to my dismay, I had loaned her my most treasured marble, which she had glibly swapped for two Sharps toffees and half a piece of Wrigley's Spearmint gum. My devastation was complete. Life Lesson Number One: Never Trust Anyone, Not Even Your Best Friend. Of course, I instantly forgot the lesson, and later in life, the marbles became men, although some of them weren't even worth the paper the toffees had been wrapped in. My next BF was my treasured neighbour in the flat downstairs. My childhood diaries written in the 'got-up-had-egg-for-breakfast' style of the day told of joint birthday parties, Sundays at the seaside, weekends in the country, swimming in the Serpentine, holidays abroad and, most importantly, trips to the museum to stare at the naked statues and try to work out what went where. We went shopping together, played Monopoly and Cluedo on rainy afternoons and went fishing in the Round Pound on our daily jaunt – entered in the diary as: 'Went to park with Sandu'. We covered for each other when shoplifting gardenia bath cubes from Woolworths (the height of olfactory sophistication in the fifties), fibbed to our parents to get the other out of trouble, swapped secrets and charm bracelets late into the night when we had sleepovers. We shared our records, our dance steps, our inability with algebra, our first experience with a razor, our discovery of our changing bodies and, once puberty hit, compared our growing boob size almost daily. (She beat me by a mile.) We mooned over Roy Orbison singing 'Only The Lonely' clutching our hairbrush mikes like we knew exactly how it felt, at age thirteen, to be dying of a broken heart. She was truly my bestest friend. Conveniently, our mothers were also great confidantes, but her parents' marriage broke up (her Italian mother used to rub the pillow with garlic to keep the English husband from coming to bed) and suddenly, at age sixteen, just when I needed her most, she was gone. The gap she left was immense and inevitably, as time passed, we lost touch. Thirty-four years later, my phone rang one evening and there she was. We picked it up like it was yesterday, reunited over a four-hour lunch and fell easily into our old speak. The unbreakable links in the chain we had forged in our childhood were renewed that afternoon, and had I still kept a diary, the entry would have read: 'Went to park with Sandu'. Our old haunts drew us back as if all the births, deaths, marriages, divorces, children and grandchildren were still waiting in our future. We retraced our indelible steps down Queensway to Kensington Gardens, through the playground, round the Round Pond, into the Orangery and back up the Broad Walk to my mother's flat for tea – two little girls inside the bodies of two worldly-wise women. It was like finding a long-lost piece of jigsaw and clicking it into place.

There are many mysteries associated with the female and her kinship. Women who live together in communes such as kibbutzniks or Mormons find their menses merging until the collected breed share a collective bleed. Women out in groups often go to the loo together, much to the mystification of their male counterparts. (We only do it to wind them up and swap lipsticks, not to cop a sly look at each other's *noonis* while we're peeing, like they do.)

God help the mister who comes between me and my sister
And God help the sister who comes between me and my
man . . .

(Irving Berlin)

Despite all the bosom buddy stuff and the 'magnanitude' women show each other in most other areas (lending her the Gucci shoes and Prada bag you haven't even worn yet because she's got a hot date; cancelling your own hot date because she's too depressed to be left alone on a Saturday night; driving to Gatwick at 4 a.m. to pick her up because her flight was delayed and the mini-cab took another fare) there is a desperately territorial possessiveness when it comes to being generous about men. The rivalry is 'daggers drawn', suspicion lurks in every smile. Even if you don't want him any more, you certainly don't want anyone else to have him (just in case you change your mind). After all, if he was yours once, he must be yours forever. You can forgive a friend who buys the identical coat to yours, goes after the job you wanted and gets it, borrows your daily help and then employs her full-time, turns up at your birthday party full of botox and breast implants, but God help her if she goes anywhere near your man. One friend I know welcomed another into her heart and home, when the latter was down and out with no prospects and nowhere to go. Helping herself to the contents of the wardrobe and the fridge was one thing, but when the guest helped herself to her hostess's husband, that was a generosity too far. The guilty parties ended up together with the betrayed wife and her child moving away in disgust. Eventually, the triangle reformed and they are all friends again with the wronged one at the apex and the other two looking up at her admiringly.

When it comes to the proliferation of men, the sad fact is (and which is sadder and 'facter' as we get older) there are never enough of them to go round (probably because as the stronger sex, we have managed to kill them all off). You only have to look at the contents of a coach heading towards Bournemouth on any sunny afternoon and you'll barely see a bald male head among the dozens of tightly permed grey ones. Ditto the old folk's homes – wall-to-wall wallflowers of widowhood as far as the eye can see. Tragically, this is where we are all headed and the losses we shall suffer, so shall we share. As you grow older and more cantankerous your patience may desert you along with your marbles and you may fall out with old friends for the most trivial of reasons, like her always wanting to lead at the Community Club tea dance or you categorically refusing to buy anything other than Pricerite's own brand digestive biscuits. So, be less dogmatic and more accepting and you will always have a friend to talk to and reminisce with throughout your twilight years. If you go ga-ga through senility or the devil dementia, then frankly, my dear, who gives a damn? You can lift your skirts above your head and dance away to your own special music.

'At last – just you and me, Tigger, and twenty-five rich, dark Belgians . . .'

8

All By Your Self

Maggi Russell

There are two tragedies in life, one is to lose your heart's desire, the other is to gain it.
        (George Bernard Shaw) (But women know better)

You can't always get what you want, but if you try some time, you just might find, you get what you need.
                (Rolling Stones) (And women usually do)

So, finally, here you are, after all the hurly burly's done, all the battles lost and won. All by yourself. Well, clever you, because *by* Your Self is a very smart place to be. It may not feel like it, right now, but yes it is, because you are also at yourself, with yourself, in yourself, even up yourself – whichever way, it can turn out to be a surprisingly cosy little bolt-hole. That said, please, please, do let's try to get *over* ourselves, because Tragic Diva is not the way to go. Finding ourselves unintentionally alone, perhaps after years in what seemed like a secure relationship, we may feel like Withnail, having gone on holiday by mistake. We never wanted to end up here, but life dragged us along when we weren't paying attention. We used to look out from our smug co-habitual nests at all our desperate single friends, and thank our lucky stars that we weren't them. And then, some evil Shakespearean curse was cast upon us, and double, double, toil and trouble, we've messed up our relationships without meaning to. Now here we are, out on the moors, Queen Lear in the howling wind. The guise of the doomed victim or wailing crone beckons. If you find yourself eyeing up speeding trains, Anna Karenina-style (so untidy) or prone to writing Plath-ian poetry (so 1960s), do stop and get a grip. Greek Tragedy, schmagedy. Maria Callas, no doubt drowning out choirs of angels as we speak, is a case in point. That God-given gift thrown away on slimming pills and some grumpy little Grecian Earner, when she could have joined the sisterhood, become a grande dame, and lived a life of operatic splendour. Yes, we may all tend towards La Traviata in our woes, but surely a little sense of proportion would add some much needed *pizzicato* to the mix. When the fat lady sings, the revelries should *begin*. We gotta fight for our right to party.

Every single person's life is a heroic quest. Each of us gets tested in a uniquely hideous and agonising way. We all have to act out our own designated little dramas. The gods design bespoke hairshirts for each and every individual. But whatever you are suffering right now, try not to see this as the end of the road. This is just the latest stage of your journey, the bit you've been trying to put off, where you finally get to go down into the underworld to confront your very own personal Minotaur. If you've had enough of wading through bullshit, never mind the claustrophobia you get on the tube, you can sign up instead with Desert Tours for forty days roaming about wailing in the wilderness, complete with ragged clothing and matted hair. Every trainee-goddess worth her starry girdle winds up facing one of these labours at some point or another.

Aristotle described tragedy as a drama arousing pity and fear. Pity is occasioned by undeserved misfortune, fear in that it has happened to someone like ourselves. Well, we all know about that, don't we?

Some women sink in the Greek fashion, and never really snap out of it. But that's also their choice. You see, they may have found that, actually, they rather like having their own space, and welcome the sheltering dark. Perhaps divorced or widowed in mid-life, facing a period at sea like the Ancient Mariner, complete with albatross neckwear of failed relationship, and nothing to put in the ship's log but grim tales of long icy moonless singles' nights, and the echoing silence emanating from frightened daughters when they suggest mooring in their harbour, many of our mothers opted instead to scupper the ship and find a warm cave, eschewing adventure and male company entirely. At the time we thought this was laziness, miserableness, or just plain spite. We realise now it was their choice, and some of those WI events were quite rockin'. My spinster aunt, never ever known to have danced the horizontal tango, nevertheless had a satisfying career, travelled the world, was always off at concerts, church events, tennis tournaments, art galleries, etc., and revelled in a life of independence. Our fixation on men is beginning to look like a curse. Maybe it wasn't just Achilles who found his soft spot to be a heel.

If a future without men is just too calamitous for you to contemplate, do please take heart. There is no reason at all to assume you won't eventually get what you really want, people generally do. It may simply be that what you thought you wanted, you didn't really, and were unconsciously trying to destroy, in the grip of a kind of emotional Munchausen's syndrome by proxy. While you were fixing his drinks and rustling up those tasty snacks, you were really cooking his goose. Your soul was plotting annihilation.

Like Steve Martin in *The Jerk*, all of our lives have their own special purpose. It may not be anything heroic on the grand scale, like solving world hunger, pacifying Islamic fundamentalists or subduing rampant capitalism. It is just as valid to concentrate on sorting yourself out, in order to stop being such a flake. Let's face it, it's probably time, don't you think? For myself, I always knew a day would come to take the path signposted Thorny Grove, away from men, away from glamour, hedonism, sex and drugs and rock 'n' roll. It simply couldn't go on for ever, it was starting to look less and less pretty. But I'm only going underground for a little while, while I sort out what has never really worked for me (overvaluing the attentions of neurotic men) and what has worked out just dandy – old friends, female friends, entertaining, autonomy, books, writing, movies, teaching, gardening, fun, shoes.

A middle-aged woman alone is often seen as a social catastrophe, lonely, eccentric, desperate, potty, outcast – especially if she lives with more than one pet. People can get quite medieval in their prejudice. Today's barbecue is yesterday's Wicker Man party. Dress code: witches – please wear inflammable nighties. (Justin! Wait your turn to throw granny on the fire!) Women are supposed to be in relationships all their lives, as daughters, sisters, wives, mothers, grannies – we're never allowed to stop looking after other people, and to prioritise number one. And yet more and more young women are living alone, and less and less are having children. The number of cats joining their households is becoming ominous. To call this a trend would be like calling Ebola a nervous rash.

We, the authors of this book, both live alone (at the time of writing!). We have (off and on) relationships a plenty – familial, sexual, animal and mineral (aka pets and jewellery) but we live alone. Sometimes we don't like it, sometimes we do. We still fantasise endlessly about meeting the dream man. We are often encouraged by tales of women alone for decades, finally finding love at sixty, seventy, eighty. Unfortunately, we are more often made downcast by tales of friends being abruptly left for blonde TV presenters at fifty. But none of this may happen. I have lots of contingency plans: to live with a girlfriend and open a cat sanctuary, to buy a big farmhouse in Tuscany with all my single mates, where we will read books to each other and stay drunk all the time, a kind of hippie commune for the Crankies with attractive young nurses. (I've recruited several men so far and they are all very keen.) Of course, it would be a nightmare to organise, because we are all too set in our ways, and all these men are single because of their disgusting habits. But I love making plans, because while I'm making them, I'm optimistic about the future.

Fear of the future is human – the uphill struggle seems never-ending. Sometimes we say we long to turn up our toes so we can just get a decent night's kip. Most people live lives of quiet desperation. All those nirvana-lite statements such as 'being grateful for each day' are impossible to live by moment by moment, life's problems are too complex, emotions are too overwhelming, there's never just one simple solution. All we can do is tolerate the uncomfortable and downright painful. Everybody hurts, sometimes. And not everyone's mojo goes on working forever (not even Mick's).

Serendipity means finding valuable things not sought for. Life is full of *them*. Discipline brings grace, self-control brings huge rewards: self-esteem, dignity, pride. And there's always so much to do.

Fight off all tendencies to be doomy about your own future. Whatever your life is like right now is just how it is right now, it says nothing at all about the future, it is not a sign or a portent. Just think of all the far-fetched stuff that has happened to you so far. There is no such thing as a meaningless life. Imagine yourself as a Queen of the Space Age – like Whoopi Goldberg in *Star Trek*. Queens of planets of the future are always at least 150 years old, yet somehow ageless and wondrously wise. (Except Klingon Queens, who have that bad forehead thing going on – how come

they haven't discovered botox by the thirty-first century?)
Just imagine you have been sent back from the future, like
the Terminator, only you are the Germinator, sent to plant
the seeds of new womanhood into middle-aged women, to
stop them colluding in the male madness that passes for
human culture, and to urge them on to take the political
reins, while leaving men to their gadgetry and games.
The Goddess, The Matriarch, The Lederene, Margaret
Thatcher – all will come again. (But with saner policies.)
If you don't fancy taking over power, at least don't compromise your values in the type of employment or the
relationships in which you engage. Middle-aged women are
just going through a bad patch, which happens to be lasting
a couple of millennia. If things get too tough, you can
always turn it into a joke. Seeing the comic potential in any
situation reverses it. What more powerful magic is there
than that?

In this in-between time (and it doesn't have to be a
*mean*time) take stock of everything you have gained. In fact,
the middle years (let's call them from forty to seventy!) or
maybe the *muddle* years, are the longest period of your life –
everyone is middle-aged longer than they are any other age.
So it really is crucial to see this time as being of especial
value, the axis on which your whole life revolves. The
middle, when you think about it, is the most satisfying part
of anything – operas, books, holidays, sex, alcoholic binges,
sandwiches. All these things may have been embarked
upon without much enthusiasm, and ended up going on too
long, making you tired, bored, or even sick. But the middle
bit was fantastic.

Howl of the She-Wolf

We live in a society built on avoidance principles and we're
all on drugs, whether it be prozac or shopping. We all know
a great deal about emotional suffering. But damping down

your life to avoid anguish leads to a neurosis worse than just feeling and handling the pain. Lugging that giant shield around could actually strain your back and do you more harm than being pierced by the arrow. (Stick with the boned corsetry, though.) What separates the wolves from the sheep in life is the capacity to endure discomfort, face fear, stare down anxiety. Maturity is all about getting the courage to live, to embrace confusion and frustration, adjust to the contrast of light and shade. Life is a never-ending game. (On a bad day you may be longing for your deathbed, so you can look back and see how it all turned out, but even that won't bring peace, because you will probably spend your last few hours pondering the paradoxes. Oscar Wilde's final words, 'This wallpaper is killing me – one of us has got to go,' shows how some people never let up on their right to ironise.) There is no easy way out once you're in the world, so forward we must go. The secret is not to get stuck, but to face the truth and soldier on. Dedicate yourself to The Real. It's very, very hard to tell the truth about life. Of course love is everything. Be loveable to be loved. Even if you end up in an old folk's home, and the ungrateful offspring rarely come to call, you can still promote the loving stuff. Those careworkers on the minimum wage who will be doing all your unsavoury little chores could do with a few laughs, and a little gratitude, instead of struggling with charges so locked in misery and regret that they become cantankerous and mean and make a lifestyle out of being difficult and lonely. Women are at the heart of the changes needed in society – at any age. Be strong like a she-wolf, and keep up the fight to be cheery.

Rethinking Men
There is a core of self that transcends femaleness, just as the concept of God transcends gender. Subconsciously, we all still think of The Creator as a man, with his beloved son, and

all his male prophets. Beards figure big. Men are tradi-
tionally the measure of things, and we have relied on their
approval for our validation. Christianity and Judaism
eradicated the original Mother Goddess and installed the
male Yahweh, who made the human race with his hands,
out of mud (typical man, taking short cuts) instead of giving
birth to them in a sea of blood like the original Goddess. The
world of work today follows male patterns – long working
hours, maximum productivity, ecological exploitation, lack
of emotionality, fear of failure, hierarchical company
structures, the dubious ethics of business deals. If the hero's
quest is towards power, the heroine's quest is towards self,
unlocking the inner voice. (Captain Pickard always follows
Whoopi's advice, no matter how illogical and pre-
menstrual sounding, because he knows her intuition is
always right. *Star Trek* is arguably the only truly post-
feminist drama on TV, with lots of totally fab female
lieutenants. If you don't know what the hell I'm talking
about, check it out on cable.) We have to re-train ourselves
to say 'no' to lots of stuff considered prizes in the male
dominion. Pleasing males means being invited to join in the
male fun and not being left out. But becoming your
authentic self may mean saying and doing stuff that
displeases both men and their brainwashed female
collaborators. In the transition period from daddy's girl to
your own woman you may mess up. It's a walk on the wild
side. When you come out of it, hopefully, you will have
developed a new relationship to the masculine, with a
positive inner male *animus* figure. No longer a chaser after
glamorous, successful but empty men, you are ready for a
man with some substance, a man with a soul.

Or you may just decide to give up men permanently.
Roseanne Barr recently announced on a chat show that she
was going celibate, because sex had 'ruined her life'. Maybe
that's true for her, and I hope it will make her happy. For

myself, going celibate is a pronouncement I would never make, partly because my friends would all scoff, but also because everyone is celibate between men – how long does that have to go on before it becomes a syndrome? Surely you would have to turn down several attractive offers before you could legitimately claim to have taken such a vow. I prefer to think that even Roseanne might eventually meet a man with a heart.

The Dark Side

Before you get there, you may have to pass through the valley of confusion, alienation, disillusion, desperation. There is no easy way out of this impasse. The simplest tasks feel Shakespearean. If Hamlet couldn't make up his mind how to solve an obvious problem (Uncle kills Dad and schtupps Mum = Kill Uncle!), how the hell can you sweat the small stuff? Turning around and running back into your old habits won't help you. It's too late, you've looked the monster in the face, and you can't pretend it wasn't ugly. During your voyage out you may be preoccupied, panicky, sad and inaccessible. You don't even want to see your best friends, let alone men. Tears are a constant – you feel abandoned. You lie on the couch watching *The Simpsons*, praying for guidance – 'Sister Marge, show me how to live!' (Don't bother with Homer, either from Springfield or from Greece – *The Odyssey* is just more guys farting about in boats, putting off going home for tea.) No, sadly you must find your own way.

Remember that little girl, who loved ponies, ballet, swimming, whatever? You are moving back to your Self, not out of yourself. You don't want to *pull yourself together*. You are dismembering, destructuring, but not destructing. This is a creative process. You are going back to your birth – and you need to do it away from men. You are reclaiming parts of yourself split off when your psyche rejected your mother and the feminine. You need to re-acquaint yourself with your body, emotions, intuition, values, pleasures. This is not a depression needing medication, but a falling apart before you put yourself back together again in a stronger, healthier, more advanced form. It's bound to be painful, because humans hate change.

Worse than the pain, maybe, is the rage. If you had a hammer, you'd hammer in the morning all right – someone's brains would be all over the fucking breakfast table. You may consider taking out a Jihad against anything with gonads. This will pass, just try to get through it without going all Fundamentalist. It's not really men's fault, they're only doing what they were told. Concentrate on yourself instead.

We all try to postpone the journey to the depths, but each time we make it we return more and more ourselves. It is not a glamorous journey, like going to Barbados, but it sure is fruitful. The dark goddess Kali awaits. Start praying to her now. She has been disabled by the notion that women should always be gentle, nurturing and sweet. This has suited patriarchy just fine. There is a need for female rage, it is what balances us. Why did you agree to become a man's doll? How did Daddy get to convince you? We became fetishised things, all boobs, anorexia and crazy shoes, walking on gilded splinters. Reclaim the feeling you had long, long ago that you could do anything you chose, walking in your ancient ancestors' sandals. Go back down to the Goddess to find your Self, and unchain her.

Try On New Hats

Where are you now? All by your new selves? With no man to whom you must show consistency in order not to freak him out, you can try out multiple new personalities now. You can be twenty-first-century schizoid woman. How you look, how you act, what you know, you can redesign it all.

Please don't think the new you has to take up Timberlands and crew-cuts. Females are beautiful by nature and deserve to be adorned all over with pretty, shiny things, like mermaids. Do consider a makeover. If you can't get Trinny and Tranny (who only style clones of themselves, anyway), get a friend with great taste to help. Changing hairstyle, make-up, clothes, all make you feel different. Beware, though, of spending a fortune doing up your home instead. Unless you are very wealthy, this can take up loads of time and effort, poring over curtains etc., and gives the self-delusion that you are changing your life, when in fact you are just burying yourself deeper in fabrics, like a hamster pulling cotton wool over its head. There is something terribly off-putting about over-designed and spotless homes – they are not inviting to guests who are afraid to move a cushion or put their feet anywhere. Better to make your nest incredibly seductive and cosy with great music, books, videos, lighting, and a well-stocked fridge Jerry Seinfeld-style, so that wacky friends are constantly dropping by.

How about getting a bit more education? It's much more rewarding to study now, than when forced to in your teens. New knowledge opens new worlds, and learning is like beauty treatments for the brain. You don't need A-levels now to graduate, the Open University runs better degrees than many of the redbricks, and invites you to crazy sex-infested summer schools as well. Or, at the very least, your Adult Ed Institute will have courses in every possible obscurity. (Wendy and I met on one!)

Don't Get Cranky

It's common to find lone middle-aged women becoming terribly finickity about diet, going on and on about weight, freaking out over the washing machine breaking down, and every little domestic drama turning into a hysterical night-mare. Of course, it is a monumental drag when the central heating or boiler dies, especially in winter. Just make sure you've got some electric heaters on standby, and adopt a siege mentality. The number of women who breezily strike up affairs with plumbers in this situation is quite extra-ordinary, and not just in porn videos. This is when you might regret that fight with the neighbours over their rubbish in your bins, or all those garden snails you chucked over the fence, because now that cup of sugar is never coming your way.

Spread Wisdom

This is the ultimate role of the older woman in society. Older men are supposed to be doing this too, but generally they remain too immature, self-obsessed and selfish to do so, and just want to remain in denial about the hair coming out of their ears. The witch is the traditional wise woman. Why she got the warty-fingered, hook-nosed raggedy image I have no idea. (Yes I have, it's male fear and prejudice.) Now all we have retained of the look is those sexy black pointy boots. (Why are pointy things sexy? Answers on a postcard please.) Wicca has much to say about woman wisdom. Why not join a coven – or start one of your own? We don't advise dancing moonclad on the heath – but an evening of candles, spells and herbal beauty treatments with the girls could be a riot. Or at least an excuse to drink some strong alcoholic potions and bake some fancy cakes. A chocolate ritual, anyone?

If you're not so flamboyantly inclined, practise saying wise and poetic things, at any given opportunity. This can freak people out a bit, so just say them flippantly, without portentous delivery. Just slip them into the conversation, all nonchalant, and watch how confused friends start to look upon you as a source of sound advice in a senseless world. (For example, 'How far that little candle throws its beams! So shines a good deed in a naughty world!' – Willy

Wonka, ex-Willy Shakespeare – everybody quotes, sometimes.) Of course you'll need actually to gain some
knowledge to turn your bird brain into a planetary one, so
just read a lot of good books and go cold turkey on trash,
and that should do the trick.

Count Your Blessings

A cliché, yes, I know, but so is feeling sorry for yourself. You
are bound to have some, if not all of the following:

Family. Hopefully you will have your children, grandchildren, or just your nephews and nieces, for the rest of
your life. (Unless you're absolutely positive you really can't
stand them, heal all rifts now!) The young will ignore you in
their teens and twenties, they're all over the place, oldies are
not cool, it's too embarrassing introducing you to new
partners when you're so tactless about the old ones. But
they all come crawling back in the end, to make sure you
haven't cut them off without a kopeck. This is also a time for
you to shuffle down memory lane with elderly relatives so
you won't regret it when they depart this mortal coil. (What
is that? How did a uterine device get into the cosmic
equation?) Daughters and mothers are particularly in need
of healing their relationships at this time. You have judged
your own harshly perchance, condemning her as needy,
self-absorbed, snobby, hypocritical? Try to have a heart,
after all, she was of the very last pre-feminist generation,
and that must has been pretty galling, watching her
daughter handed everything on a plate, while she had to
put up and shut up about so much. If they seem bitchy,
jealous, retrogressive, how might you have turned out in the
same circumstances? They can't *all* have set out on a
deliberate mission to fuck their children up. Discouraged
from education or careers, they then had to cope with war,
rationing, husbands off abroad carousing with 'Allo 'Allo'
fillies, only to be followed by the hideous tranked-out fifties,

after their own little Führers came trooping home again. (Rubber girdles? Mascara mixed with spit? *Mangling*? Read Betty Friedan, and *frisson* to the horror.) Your mother is the most significant person you'll ever know. I'm afraid she is never going to leave you, even after she is dead. She will just move herself into your head, and express herself in every little thing you do – your tone of voice, your little homilies, that weird involuntary grimace, the messy way you peel potatoes. Make your peace, try to understand her needy love, talk to her before it's too late, tell her you finally understand now, even if secretly, you don't.

Friends. These now truly earn their weight in gold. Friends are arguably the most valuable currency of all. To think we ever even contemplated betraying them for men! Single men usually get increasingly lonely as they age, while women have more mates than ever. If only we were lesbians, we'd be in heaven. And there are always opportunities to make new ones. Fill your life with all the affectionate, humorous, wise and sympathetic company you crave. Not just hetero-sexuals – find some gay friends too, and companions of every age group. Personally, I adore being an ersatz mother to my young girlie protégées, cooing over their pregnancies, reading their tea leaves (they're terribly gullible), revelling in crackpottiness as they soak up all my queer advice and half-baked theories, smothering them in bosomy sympathy and creamy puddings. Steering well clear of their own mums for the usual reasons, they lap it all up, fantasise about getting me off with their dads, and lavish me with praise for my wafty, witchy, womanly ways. It can be such a relief not to be the subject anymore, to stand back and let young girls be the vessels of beauty, to no longer see them as a threat, to join the rest of the human race in appreciating them, to com-pliment them for their loveliness, and pay them respect, just for existing. I told a girl on the tube the other day that she was gorgeous, just for the heck of it, because she was such a pleasure to look at. No wonder men stare and comment – except the way they do it is so predatory. She seemed shyly pleased, and certainly didn't think I was trying to be funny.

Work. This is the time to make like Spiderwoman and get weaving your web. Networking is second nature to women. If you're not in paid employment that you love, and you need to work, you can start a business at any age – especially after retirement when you've got time to indulge any fantasy, and perhaps with no old man to distract you. If you are of a creative bent, consider turning your writing, painting, pottery or sewing into cash. Mary Wesley, the successful novelist, wrote her first book at seventy-two. Putting yourself on the job market can be very disheartening after fifty, when so few industries value your wisdom and experience. Many women go into alternative therapies and teaching. Voluntary work, too, can be very rewarding – victim support groups, Third World and AIDS charities, hospices – all will welcome your input with open arms.

The people you meet doing this type of work tend to be really kind people, too, and it's much more fun than it sounds. You could train as a counsellor at any age, a fascinating job. At the very least, you could visit old people in your neighbourhood, the pleasure this gives is incalculable. The reward to yourself is almost like being in love, as you receive so much affection and gratitude from others. Of course, you can only do this if you have time – the minute you feel like a martyr is the time to stop, so don't pressure yourself. But now you can truly become a productive and useful part of society, turning all that powerful woman energy into changing the world. The big global issues are much too complex to tackle head on, and society is far too fragmented for generalised solutions. So, unless you are Glenda Jackson (Hallo Glenda!) think small and find a political pressure group with an agenda that interests you.

There are enough *isms* out there for each and every one of us. If the thought of no longer working for glamour, money, fame or prestige depresses you, then fine, you are not ready. Carry on with your high-profile career until you drop – just make sure this will be when you are good and ready, and not when your organs prematurely pack up.

Creativity. Writing, painting, pottery, interior design, dress design, gardening, cookery, music – make like Sister Rosetta and her electric guitar, start a rock band called Granny Takes a Trip – or just focus on spiritual exploration. You've got time now to take all those classes you've been meaning to take, or even to teach one – a great method for improving your social life, as students always like to suck up to teacher.

Write Your Life Story

Draw your lifeline on a piece of paper, from birth to the present, and divide it up into relevant periods, perhaps around significant events (such as marriages, relationships, births, jobs, house moves). Give each period places, people and activities that were important. Below the line, write the tone of the period. Try to think what is the tone of the period you are in right now? If it's negative, resolve to do something about it, so that when you move into the next period, you will see this as one of pivotal change. Another fascinating little exercise I give my writing students is to construct a fairy story about their own lives. It helps to give your life a shape, to see it as a kind of myth with a meaning. Here's the basic structure: something happened so that a character had a problem and a need, then a struggle ensued, which led to a crisis, that was finally resolved when a transformation took place. See how you can fit your own life into this schema. (I've never yet met a person without a problem and a need!) Then write a letter to a present or future grandchild telling them the one major thing you have learned from your life. This will help to clarify your own little drama, and help you to envisage its resolution. (And its much cheaper than therapy.)

Eventually – Androgyny?

This comes about through the union of opposites, and is actually a transcendent state.

Inside every person there is an interplay of both male and female qualities, becoming more androgynous means recognising the unconscious 'other' inside your soul. This does not mean becoming neuter. The more feminine you become, the more masculine too. Everything gets stronger and more defined, the two opposing qualities are not working against each other, cancelling each other out, making you a neither, but you can utilise all the human gifts of male and female to create something electrifyingly powerful and free – an integrated androgyny. For myself, I see becoming more male as an absolute positive. I have never understood men at all. My own male child is sensitive, gentle and affectionate. How do they get from this to the heartless, ruthless, unemotional adult males we have to deal with today? Read Alon Gratch's *If Men Could Talk . . . This is what they would say*, to find out. (If I could care, what I would say is ****!!***?!) It seems that society brutalises them, and hurts them so badly, they become stunted and damaged like rejected EC courgettes, swearing never to fully love another human being again. And so they don't, and treat women like sex commodities. Women hanker, chase, whine and demand explanations. Please, just don't. Walk away from heartbreak and don't look back. Don't phone, don't ask for closure, don't post-mortemise. Be like Clint, saddle up your high horse, wear a poncho (very fashionable again), ride out of town. Look forward, think: where can I go to cause some trouble next? Men move on, throw themselves into a new project, get into a new relationship, and don't think about you at all, anymore. One man told me he still dreams about a certain ex, and thinks about her nostalgically (men can be very sentimental), but he wouldn't dream of calling her up or wanting to see her. It's finished business, next! The only piece of unimpeachable advice I have ever gleaned from a lifetime of reading women's magazines is this: THE ONLY REASON MEN DON'T PHONE IS BECAUSE THEY DON'T WANT TO. Especially these days, when everyone has a mobile, and even hospitals have phones they can wheel to his bedside. Please, let's just stop all the self-delusion. Unfortunately, he didn't fall into a coma, nor is he beside himself with grief over his mother's sudden demise. He's in a bar or a bed somewhere, *with someone else.* Women can never finish anything – we do everything in a circular fashion, going round and round, over and over the same ground. (Just watch how men and women mow lawns.) Be linear, move along, eyes to the horizon. This is the new androgyny – using what is productive in your masculine side, without the constant belching or taking books into the loo. Feminism has done this huge great valuable thing – teaching us to value our female ways. It's also done a truly terrible thing, making us as vulgar as men. We can incorporate the best of all that virile male stuff, while retaining our graceful, tasteful, foxy ways.

Survive
This is ultimately all we are here to do, and the winners are the ones who do it without too much moaning. That is the meaning of the game, to see who can get through it all in a good mood. You lose points for railing at fate, the gods, the young, the government, for wearing polyester and that sour expression. Every day you are alive and not in pain is a day you have won, because you survived yesterday. If you actually are in physical pain, then you have a burden way beyond the rest of us spineless and spoon-fed individuals

who whine on about the price of everything, knowing the value of nothing. (Got to give Oscar the penultimate word, 'cause no one knew better than him how to go out on a high.) If you can just survive your own life and crack a few good jokes along the way, you are on to something big.

And remember, mustn't crumble . . .

(Draw your own)
Conclusion

Wendy Salisbury

To all the men I've loved before
Who wandered in and out my door
For helping me to grow
I owe a lot, I know
To all the men I've loved before . . .

A Hammond/H Davis

If any men have actually got through this book without hurling it at the wall or forming a posse and coming after us like a lynch mob, we feel we owe you an explanation. We know there are some good men out there – between us we married and divorced several of them. The tales we have told have been taken from our own and others' Real Life Experiences and although there are three sides to every story – his, hers and the truth – we could not compromise our integrity by sugar-coating ours.

No men were harmed in the writing of this book. Many were discussed, derided, disbelieved, discredited, disqualified, disinfected, distended, dishevelled, discharged, dismayed and dispatched. Most, save a dismal few, were dispensable.

Guys, we know we have been tough on you but that is how you have made us. Repression has led to aggression, whose fault is that? Right now, it's true, we are more ourselves than ever before. You may find this scary. With crampons, ropes and pulleys, we have climbed the mountain of our lives and do not intend to fall arse over tit down the other side. The wisdom we have gained through facing our challenges head-on will be channelled into a solid base on which to build our futures. Some of us may have another fifty years left, since thanks to medical science, our life expectancy has increased by two years in every decade since the twenties. This means that if life were a bottle of shampoo, we now get an extra 20 per cent free! We are turning our knowledge into energy to power the next period and make it the most productive yet. We are not in our second childhood, we are embarking on a second life, often *sans* partner. We taught our kids how to rock 'n' roll, shop and have sex. Elvis, The Beatles and the Stones wrote and sang their songs just for us. The sixties and seventies styles our children now wear were designed around our nubile bodies, and the Pill was invented to give us our sexual freedom. Advertisers should wise up and stop only targeting twenty- and thirty-somethings with their ads for drink, fashion and cars. We drink cocktails, wear funky clothes and drive fast cars too. We are not about to disappear upstairs in a Stannah stairlift to check the water in our walk-in bath or renew our life insurance.

It may not seem from our rantings and ramblings that we like men at all, but this is SO not so. If we did not like them, we would not have wasted the past year writing about them. We're just looking to retrain them to make them more agreeable to live with. In a way – though it may not seem so – this book is a *hommage* to men, and by reading it and taking note of how things are from *our* perspective, it might teach them to behave better and treat us with the honour and respect that we deserve. If any men have something to say, we'd love to hear it. We would welcome their side of any story, to redress the balance from their point of view. Alternatively, why not fess up and admit that your primary reason for living is to get your end away and that you know you have dished out some pretty abysmal behaviour in the pursuit of this activity? Just remember that as you grow older, when someone offers you super sex, you'll be more likely to opt for the soup.

We live in hope, how else is there to live? I (WS) have recently met two or three charming new men, who do not drag their pasts around with them like sacks of rotten potatoes and beat other women over the head with them. Men are as keen to move on as we are, and know that, God willing, they have much to offer the right woman for the rest of both their lives. Maggi has cleared a place in her head and her heart and is pursuing her career, her son's upbringing and her solid belief that from out there, somewhere, The One will come.

If you 'gentlemen' care to share, then fine – if not (stand by for Gloria Gaynor moment): WE WILL SURVIVE. The road, however, is long and we would welcome a hand to hold as we walk along it. The most important thing in all the world is that *we want to love you, and we want you to love us.* And we know that deep down inside you do . . . because we know how to make really good chocolate brownies . . . And you like those, don't you?

Bibliography

Campbell, Joseph. *The Hero with a Thousand Faces*. Fontana Press (1993)

Coelho, Paulo. *The Alchemist*. HarperCollins (1992)

Freke, Timothy and Gandy, Peter. *Jesus and the Goddess*. Thorsons (2002)

Gafni, Marc. *Soul Prints*. Penguin (2001)

Gratch, Alon, Ph.D. *If Men Could Talk . . . This is what they would say*. Arrow Books (2001)

Graves, Robert. *The White Goddess*. Faber & Faber (1997)

Griffin, Susan. *The Book of the Courtesans*. Broadway Books (2001)

Jung, CJ. *Modern Man in Search of a Soul*. Routledge (2001)

Jung, CJ. *Psychology and Alchemy*. Routledge (2000)

Murdock, Maureen. *The Heroine's Journey*. Shambhala Publications Inc. (1990)

Northrup, Dr Christiane. *Women's Bodies, Women's Wisdom*. Judy Piatkus (Publishers) Ltd. (2001)

Ragan, Kathleen. *Fearless Girls, Wise Women and Beloved Sisters*. W.W. Norton & Co. Inc. (2000)

Rogers, Rita. *Soul Mates, A Practical, Spiritual Guide to Finding True Love*. Pan Books (2000)

Sova, Dawn B. Ph.D. *The Encyclopedia of Mistresses*. Robson Books (2001)

Tannahill, Reay. *Sex in History*. Scarborough Press (1992)

Whitmont, Edward C. *Return of the Goddess*. Continuum (1997)

Acknowledgements

Thanks to: Tina B (for 25 years on the hotline), Stephie, Alison, Joan, Gillie, Merril, Nikki (for laughing at my attempts to be a lesbian), Sheila and Chris, Dinah and Peter, Pat and Neil (for keeping my faith in couples), TDN ('til death do us part though it sticks in my craw), Mark R (for the name and the beetles), Mr O for the R 'n' R, Andy M. for techno support, James for cuddles, and Wendy for being the E that squares the M.

Maggi Russell

With effusive thanks to my much-loved support system for baring, daring and sharing: Adrianne, Annie, Brenda, Briege, Dorothy, Jill, Jude, Nikki and Sonya.

To my big sister Marilyn: the saint by the seaside, to the Supercrinks Min and Ned, and of course to The Plum, my NBF forever.

And to Eddie, Joe, Mel, Roger and Suave Harve for always being just a phone call away.

Wendy Salisbury

And of course thanks to Jeremy Robson and Jane Donovan at Robson Books and to John Needleman, who made it happen.

Maggi Russell

Wendy Salisbury